TAUNTON'S

LAWN
GUIDE

TAUNTON'S
LAWN
GUIDE

Maintaining a GREAT-LOOKING Yard

JOHN FECH

The Taunton Press

 **The Taunton Press**
Inspiration for hands-on living™

The Taunton Press, Inc., 63 South Main Street, PO Box 5506, Newtown, CT 06470-5506
e-mail: tp@taunton.com

Distributed by Publishers Group West

EDITOR: Roger Yepsen
COVER DESIGN: Ann Marie Manca
INTERIOR DESIGN: Jonathan Walker
LAYOUT: Lori Wendin
ILLUSTRATOR: Mona Mark

Library of Congress Cataloging-in-Publication Data
Fech, John C.
    Taunton's lawn guide : maintaining a great-looking yard / John Fech.
        p. cm.
    ISBN 1-56158-520-3
    1. Lawns. I. Title.
    SB433 .F43 2002
    635.9'647--dc21   2002009350

Printed in the United States of America
10 9 8 7 6 5 4 3 2 1

The following manufacturers/names appearing in *Taunton's Lawn Guide* are trademarks: Ariens®, Deere®, Embark®, eXmark®, Finale®, *Fine Gardening*®, Honda Power Equipment®, *Horticulture*®, Hunter®, IBDU®, MTD®, Primo®, ProMow®, Rain Bird®, Roundup®, Scotts®, Seedland®, Snapper®, Toro®, Trimec®, Tupersan®, and Weed-B-Gon®.

Acknowledgments

THIS BOOK HAS SIMPLY BEEN A LABOR OF LOVE in every sense of the phrase. I'd like to thank my family for their support and encouragement. Their heartfelt message to me has always been, "You can do it! You're my (kid, husband, dad)!" A big thank you also goes to my editor, Roger Yepsen, who helped turn my ramblings into a clear, concise tome. Thanks to Jennifer Renjilian, Suzanne Noel, and Rosalind Wanke at The Taunton Press, for giving *Taunton's Lawn Guide* readability and a great presentation.

Through the years, I've been fortunate to have received instruction, support, and encouragement from a great many people including Drs. J. Ackland Jones, Donald Steinegger, Roch Gaussoin, Tom Fermanian, Robert Shearman, and Edward Kinbacher and Professor Donald Janssen. These colleagues have been alongside at various stages of my career and provided invaluable assistance and guidance.

Contents

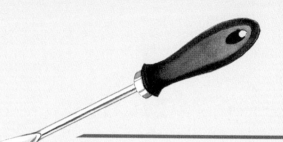

Introduction

T HERE'S NOTHING MORE WELCOMING to the eyes—and the feet—than a lush, green carpet of grass. Envision this scenario: You walk out onto your patio on a Saturday morning, cup of coffee in hand, still barefoot and full of ideas for the day ahead. The lawn looks inviting. You take a step out onto it. The grass feels soft and supple between your toes and cool to your feet.

A healthy lawn is more than just a pleasant backdrop. It provides a place to be active without walls. It traps dust and generates oxygen. It helps absorb the noise of traffic. It prevents erosion. A good-looking lawn increases property values. Small wonder that for the great majority of us, a lawn is an integral part of what we call home.

Although this book is concerned with a particular short, green plant, I begin by talking about landscaping—the ways in which lawns fit into an overall plan. After all, chances are your yard isn't exclusively devoted to grass. In deciding whether a part of your property should be devoted to lawn or to something else, I suggest following the simple rule of "Right plant, right place." Any plant will thrive if grown in a place suited to it. This book guides you in two ways: determining which parts of the yard are best for lawn, then choosing the particular cultivars of grass.

Once you've made these choices, I suggest that you take an active approach to lawn care. Otherwise, mowing and other lawn-care tasks can become a boring chore, something to be put off as long as possible.

Your idea of a great weekend may not be seeding, fertilizing, and mowing, but there are proven ways to go about lawn care that take surprisingly little time. It all begins with deciding just how involved you want to be, and I'll suggest how to go about that.

You can have an attractive low-maintenance lawn by planning it to be that way, not just by allowing the grass to tend to itself. Or, if you prefer a high-maintenance carpet that will be the envy of your neighbors, there's a systematic approach for that, too. How about the moderate, middle path that yields a presentable lawn with modest effort? There are certain grasses and practices that will get you there, as well.

Will this book make lawn care fun? That depends on your idea of a good time. If you enjoy spending several hours outdoors each month, helping nature to create a garden setting for your family, then the answer is "yes." I'll offer well-planned regimens that are very satisfying to carry out. And there is the added incentive of knowing that your yard is a highly public display of the way you feel about your home.

1

How to Use This Book

THIS BOOK IS DESIGNED to make it easy to find what you need to know. The first five chapters of the book detail the planning, preparation, and tasks you need to follow to get a great lawn. Instructions are described in the text, accompanied by photos and drawings.

There are also other elements, such as sidebars, to help you understand the process or the tools better, find smarter ways to accomplish a task, and quickly see what you need for each process.

The sidebars explain aspects in more depth and give reasons for a particular task. In some cases, they'll explain alternatives to the processes described in the main text. The sidebars are meant to help, but they're not essential to understanding the process or completing the task.

Tool Talk sidebars teach you more about the tools you'll need for the job and help you decide which tool to buy. What You'll Need sidebars are like a recipe ingredients list. They tell you what equipment

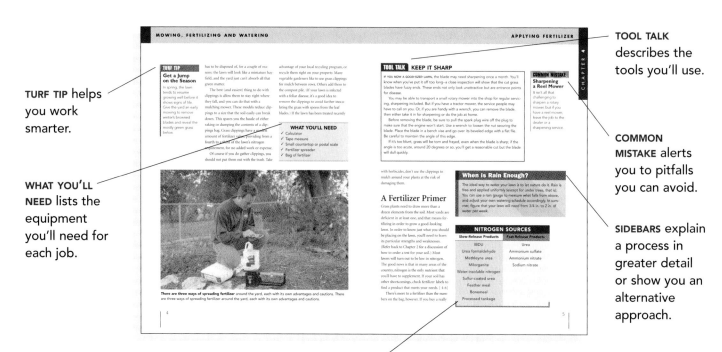

TURF TIP helps you work smarter.

WHAT YOU'LL NEED lists the equipment you'll need for each job.

TOOL TALK describes the tools you'll use.

COMMON MISTAKE alerts you to pitfalls you can avoid.

SIDEBARS explain a process in greater detail or show you an alternative approach.

CHARTS list information in an easy-to-read format.

you'll need before you begin one of the projects.

Turf Tips and Common Mistakes bring you the expertise of an author with years of experience. Turf Tips are ideas or insights that will save you time or money. Common Mistakes alert you to common misconceptions so you can make better decisions about the right lawn-care plan for your yard.

The last three chapters contain all of these elements as well as extensive charts to make it easy for you to find the information you need. In chapter 6, you'll find a comprehensive list of the most common problems you'll encounter in your lawn, from insects to diseases to weeds. In chapter 7, you'll find a list of the most common grasses—their qualities and where they grow best—to help you choose the right grass for your lawn. And in chapter 8, you'll find a calendar for every region of the country to help you identify when to do all of the tasks your lawn requires.

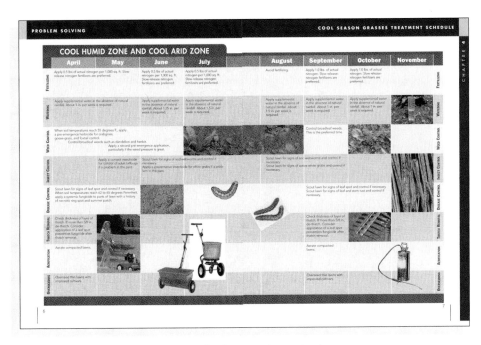

CALENDARS tell what to do and when.

Getting to Know Your Yard

Coming Up with a Plan

Keeping Lawns on Their Own Turf

Choosing Your Maintenance Level

Hiring a Landscape Pro

SURVEYING THE YARD

GOOD LAWNS ARE PART OF A GOOD LANDSCAPE PLAN. No, this isn't a book on landscaping, but we can't talk about one without the other. Your overall goal, after all, is to surround the home with beautiful, healthy plants. Having a beautiful lawn is largely about making the right choices—placing grass and ornamentals in the right locations, choosing the right grass for your conditions, and planting a lawn that requires only the time and energy you want to devote to it. If you make considered choices for your lawn, you're on your way to a beautiful landscape.

Getting to Know Your Yard

I find that most homeowners tend to assume that grass can be grown just about anywhere. Well, it can—but not well. In fact, grass plants are just as dependent on location as flowers and vegetables. Although your exist-ing lawn may be growing in the most logical places, chances are a few areas would be bet-ter off without grass, while at least one bed of ornamentals or shrubbery might look and function better as lawn. So, try to think of the yard as a blank slate, even if you've lived in the same place for 20 years.

To get started, step outside and look at your yard as if you've never seen it before. (If you're just moving in and have nothing but bare ground to contemplate, new lawns are covered in chapter 3.) Simply walk around with an open mind.

Learn a bit about your lawn's needs, and you'll be rewarded with a home landscape that looks good year-round.

- Make mental notes about how this landscape would look with different arrangements of lawn, ground covers, trees, flower beds, and built features such as a patio, arbor, or deck.

- Instead of thinking of specific plants you'd like to see, visualize general shapes and forms of plant material; it may help to squint your eyes, as landscape painters do when studying a view.

- Into this scene, imagine the various activities that your family likes to engage in—touch football, backyard barbeques, sunbathing, reading, gardening, or running with the dog.

This is a pretty simple exercise, but most of us take our yards for granted and barely notice them when we step outside. For a better-looking yard, you have to know just

The Eco-Friendly Lawn

Is a green, healthy-looking lawn a good thing for the environment or a bad thing? There is some concern that lawn-care chemicals may leach through the soil or run off the lawn and cause groundwater pollution. But a properly sited and maintained lawn is an asset to the environment, not a detriment. Here are some of its benefits:

- **Oxygen.** A 25-ft. by 25-ft. lawn produces enough oxygen to sustain one person.

- **Temperature.** In summer, an average front lawn can have the cooling effect of two or three whole-house air-conditioning units.

- **Pollution.** A lawn absorbs gaseous pollutants, such as carbon dioxide, and traps dust and dirt from the air.

- **Fire retardation.** A buffer zone of grass helps prevent fire from spreading to homes and outbuildings.

- **Water quality.** The lawn's layers of thatch and roots act to prevent soil erosion and to filter contaminants from rainwater.

Call In a Neighborhood Consultant

Ask a friend with an attractive lawn to join you for a stroll around your property. Ask for suggestions, with a clipboard in hand to record any ideas that strike you as helpful.

For a fresh perspective on the home landscape, you might also ask if you can view your yard from a neighbor's roof or (a little more safely) a top-story window. The point of this odd-sounding request is that it is much easier to understand your lawn's layout from well above ground level. Again, bring along a clipboard to sketch any potential improvements that catch your eye.

Should You Start Over?

If your lawn looks bad no matter how you've worked to bring it back to health and vigor, then you may be faced with having to start over. Don't blame yourself. Some-times lawns just go astray. An uncontrollable disease or insect outbreak might ravage the grass. Or, you may be a new homeowner, confronted with a lawn that suffers from the previous owner's mistakes.

So, what to do? First, inventory the lawn as described below in order to assess the situation. You'll be killing off the existing grasses (and weeds) and dealing with the lawn as a blank slate. Now is your chance to set problems right:

- Take care of drainage problems by amending the soil or putting in a drainage system.

- If the soil is heavy and compacted, incorporate organic matter before reseeding.

- If the lawn has been choked by an accumulation of thatch, thin it now.

- This may or may not be the best time to deal with pests or diseases because they often respond well to treatment only in certain seasons (see chapter 6).

When considering the best cultivar or mix of grasses with which to reseed, look for choices that will address problems you've had in the past. For example, if the lawn is thin due to shade, switch to fescues, St. Augustinegrass, or centipedegrass. If white grubs are devastating the lawn, you might do better with a deeper-rooted grass species such as tall fescue or buffalograss. If summer patch is an annual source of headaches, use disease-resistant seed instead of common cultivars.

---

what it is you're working with—both its limitations and any strong points worth preserving.

Coming Up with a Plan

After this casual tour, it's time to arm your-self with a clipboard and go through a four-step process that will be your guide to making your lawn the best it can be.

Step 1. Do an inventory

Begin by sketching an informal map of the site. With a blank piece of paper on your clipboard, rough-in the driveway, the house, the patio, and any other structures that are not likely to change in the next five years. (If you have access to the property's plat or survey, you can base the map on it.) Next, note the site's qualities on the map. Here are the things I look for when I visit a yard:

- **Lawn.** Look for off-colored grass and thin, worn-out areas, as well as thriving sections of lawn. Check to see if falling leaves are smothering nearby lawn.

- **Slopes.** Grass can hug a slope quite well but tends to look shaggy or worn.

- **Sunlight.** Observe the shadows in the morning, at noon, and again in the evening. The sun may not necessarily shine where you expect it to at various times of the day. The season of the year also greatly influences the length and placement of shadows.

- **Soils.** Identify areas where the soil is powdery or dusty and the plants are strug-gling. Also note any spots where water tends to collect after a rain and whether there are cracks or ruts in the ground.

- **Groupings of ornamentals.** Look for blotches on the leaves, plants that produce

SEASONAL SHADOWS

WINTER SUN

← South

SUMMER SUN

← South

some leaves but don't flower, and plants that aren't growing vigorously.

- **Vegetable gardens.** Record whether plants are healthy and producing well or spindly and showing signs of disease.

Step 2. Do an analysis

Now, write down your best guesses on why these parts of the yard look the way they do. Use a different color pen or pencil to make this analysis stand out from the inventory you just completed.

Together, these two sets of details will help you choose the best plants and grass cultivars. (A cultivar is a fancy-sounding name for a plant variety; for example, Kentucky bluegrass *Poa pratensisis* is one of several grass species.) You may be a fan of creeping red fescue, but it won't survive long in hot afternoon sun, and the inventory and analysis process will keep you from making the expensive and time-consuming mistake of using this species for a sun-baked location. Here are some things to consider when evaluating your existing site:

- **Lawn.** Off-colored, thin, or worn-out areas may indicate the wrong choice of grass cultivar. Refer to "Lawns for Active Kids" on p. 38 to learn more about the

best species for high-traffic areas. If fallen leaves are a problem, either plan on being more vigilant with the rake or plant the area to a ground cover that doesn't need pampering, such as pachysandra or ivy.

- **Slopes.** Grass on slopes may be difficult to get at with a lawn mower. And slopes often take a beating when kids coast down them on bikes and sleds. A traditional wall of stone—or one made of landscaping ties—offers more visual interest than a grassy slope. This will involve cutting and filling: taking soil from the lower end of the slope and

YARD INVENTORY

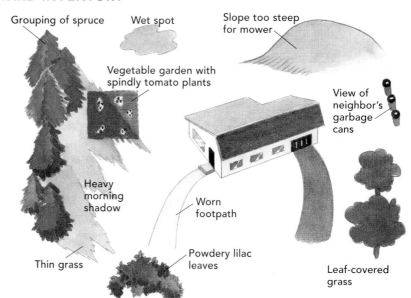

Grouping of spruce

Wet spot

Slope too steep for mower

Vegetable garden with spindly tomato plants

View of neighbor's garbage cans

Heavy morning shadow

Worn footpath

Thin grass

Powdery lilac leaves

Leaf-covered grass

TURF TIP

Turf versus Trees

Few grasses do well with less than three to five hours of direct sunlight, and trees can hog most of the sun before it reaches the ground. So replace light-starved areas of the lawn with such denizens of the dark as hostas, sansevieria, lamium, lilyturf, and English ivy.

transferring it to the top for an abrupt change of grade.

- **Sunlight.** If trees or buildings block all direct sunlight from a section of lawn for several hours each day, then you may be better off with shade-adapted grasses such as St. Augustinegrass or fine fescue. Chapter 7 will help you pick out the best grass for these sites. The number of hours of sun are critical for the performance of other plants as well. For example, viburnums won't flower and burning bush (euonymus) won't turn red in the fall if they are not located in full sun.

- **Soils.** Powdery, dusty soil may be getting enough water but allowing the water to seep away too quickly. You can aerate the ground for improved penetration, install in-ground sprinklers, or simply get out there and water a little more often. Standing water will cause most plants to struggle, due to low oxygen levels around

the roots. Consider changing larger areas to a pond or planting a mini-wetland with reeds, rushes, sedges, and cattails. Alternatively, see chapter 2 for ideas on improving the drainage to allow growing grass. Cracks and ruts from lawn-mower wheels usually indicate the soil is too hard to support good root growth.

- **Groupings of ornamentals.** Blotches on the leaves are a possible sign of foliar disease or the shrubs may simply need a good pruning to increase airflow. Plants that produce some leaves but don't flower or look thrifty may be affected by pathogenic diseases, or they may have been plunked down in the wrong place.

- **Vegetable gardens.** If the plants look healthy enough and the garden receives eight hours of sun each day, then leave the garden as it is now. However, if the area gets only three hours of sun and the plants are pale, covered with mildew, or

YARD SOLUTIONS

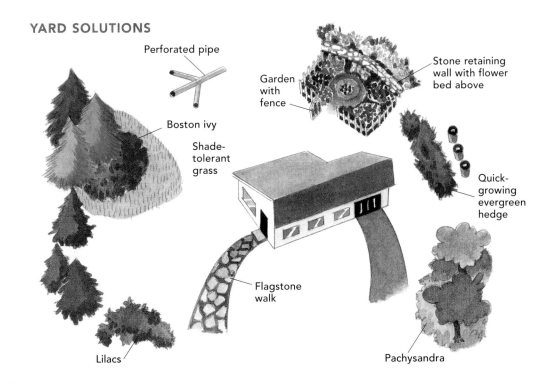

Perforated pipe

Garden with fence

Stone retaining wall with flower bed above

Boston ivy

Shade-tolerant grass

Quick-growing evergreen hedge

Flagstone walk

Lilacs

Pachysandra

producing disappointing yields, then it's a good idea to plant the garden to a shade-adapted ground cover or species of grass.

Step 3. Locate areas for lawns and gardens

After the inventory and analysis notes are down on paper, lay a sheet of translucent paper on top for this next step. It's time to decide how each area of the yard would be best used.

Areas that are in full sun, mostly flat, and well drained tend to be good places to grow a lawn. Using a pencil, outline these areas to make simple lawn shapes in what horticulturalists and architects alike call "bubbles." Try to avoid creating long, narrow, linear, or strictly geometric bubbles for lawns, unless you desire a formal yard; these shapes are hard to water, fertilize, and mow. Feel free to

erase and start over if your first tries don't seem pleasing. (Even accomplished landscape designers will experiment with several shapes when sketching lawn areas.) Pick a color with which to shade in the bubbles.

What should you do with the other areas? Consider alternatives such as ground covers, ornamental grasses, perennial flowers, and shrubs. In this way, you may arrive at a yard that looks far more interesting and also requires fewer hours of maintenance each week. Built features can help as well. A shady spot might be just the place for a patio. Replace a slope in the lawn with a wall, and you'll have the side benefit of two picturesque spots for flower beds: above and below the change of grade. Or a slope could be broken up with a terrace. Indicate each of these nonlawn areas with its own color.

Finally, you may want to shuffle plants to locations where they'll be happier. For

Small, oddly shaped nooks of the yard are difficult to water, aerate, power-rake, and fertilize evenly. These spots cause waste and pollution, so they are logical places for ornamentals.

11

Curving contours add interest to a lawn and provide an opportunity to plan attractive steps and walls.

An Important Rule

When plotting the future of your yard, a 25-ft. tape measure will help you get an accurate idea of its scale. That's particularly important in narrow areas because strips of yard less than 5 ft. in width may prove difficult to maintain as lawn.

example, if the vegetable garden isn't in full sun, designate a new area for it in a part of the landscape that is free of shade most of the day.

Step 4. Choose a grass species

Finally, you're ready to select the plants, including one or more types of lawn grass. Each cultivar of grass has an ideal set of conditions that, if met in your yard, will allow it to thrive—even if you don't consider yourself to have a green thumb. Use the notes from the inventory and analysis to select

from the grasses in terms of sun, shade, traffic, disease or insect problems, soil conditions, and slope of the land. Chapter 7 will guide you through the choices.

For example, if your lot (or your neighbor's) has several large shade trees, your inventory may note that most of the backyard receives only three to four hours of sunlight each day—meaning that grasses that need high light levels, such as bermudagrass and Kentucky bluegrass, are not good choices. Instead, begin your search by considering tall fescue and St. Augustinegrass.

Some grasses do better than others on a slope, which can be a challenge for fainter species.

There is no one super-grass that will thrive in any light condition. Switch species in areas that receive few hours of sunlight each day.

COMMON MISTAKE
Using Lawn as a Filler

Avoid the common "turf everywhere" approach, in which trees and shrubs are planted first and grass is used to fill in the spaces. The result is a landscape where the grass looks like an afterthought, rather than an integral, planned part of the design.

Keeping Lawns on Their Own Turf

The areas you identify as suitable for lawn or ground cover, referred to as *voids* in landscaping terminology, should be thought of as distinct from *masses* of grouped shrubs, flowers, and trees. The contrast of mass and void is a very powerful landscape design technique. Many of the suburban lawns I see don't take advantage of it. You probably know what I mean—tidy yards of lush grass, with specimen trees set out at regular intervals and six packs of petunias placed in neat rows.

Begin by identifying the best locations for lawn, and only then decide on ornamentals to place around these areas. By separating the two types of plantings, you make each more attractive. Generous expanses of lawn are much more pleasing to the eye if they are definable, with an obvious start and stop.

The separation of lawns and ornamentals is important for practical reasons as well. When it comes to taking care of the landscape, the two have quite different maintenance needs. In general, lawns require much more water, fertilizer, and general care than ornamentals do. (See the sidebar on the facing page for the relative hierarchy of landscape plants.)

If lawn and ornamental plants are intermingled, they'll receive the same levels of water, fertilizer, and pesticides by default, which is not good—ornamentals can get too much of a good thing. Excessive water tends to cause their roots to develop rot diseases. Too much fertilizer can lead to abundant foliar growth, which sounds like a benefit but actually causes problems for ornamentals. Nitrogen, in particular, tends to cause the leggy, floppy growth that is attractive to many pests. Additionally, leaf growth comes at the expense of carbohydrate storage and

POWER OF MASS AND VOID IN THE LANDSCAPE

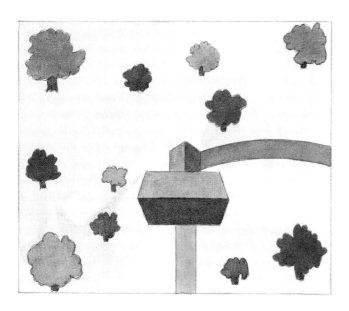

AN INEFFECTIVE GROUPING

A DYNAMIC GROUPING

MAINTENANCE LEVELS FOR PLANTS

Here are the various types of plants grown in the suburban land-scape, listed from most to least maintenance intensive. Note that the most prevalent—grass—is the most demanding, which explains why the number-one leisure activity for many of us homeowners is lawn care.

Most Work	Least Work
Lawn grass	Ground covers
Plants trained to shapes (espalier, topiary)	Evergreen and deciduous shrubs
	Evergreen trees
Annual and perennial flowers	Deciduous trees

A lawn looks its best if seen against a backdrop of ornamentals. Plan your yard so that the placement of both lawn and ornamentals is clearly intentional.

By keeping grass apart from trees, shrubs, and ground cover, you can greatly reduce the time you spend on caring for each.

Some landscape spaces just aren't meant for turf. But you can exploit these areas for shaded patios or beds of shade-loving plants.

root growth, both of which are vital to the plant. This mismatch of requirements is especially serious if you are meeting the needs of a medium- to high-maintenance lawn (a concept discussed later); adjacent flowers and shrubs will likely get an overdose and begin to decline.

Another reason for separating lawn from ornamentals has to do with you and your family. It's pretty difficult to practice soccer with your kids in a backyard choked with trees, shrubs, and flower beds. The same is

Trees are protected by their bark, but that doesn't mean they can stand up to run-ins with a mower. Maintain a grass-free circle around trees, planting it to a ground cover or mulching it.

true for any outside activity that calls for wide open spaces—laying boards aside as you build a new deck, drying out wet camping gear, or shooting off fireworks on the Fourth of July.

Tough places to grow turf

As versatile as lawn grasses may be, there are locations where they just won't flourish. In general, a lawn needs at least five hours of sun each day, a large uninterrupted area, well-drained soil, and a relatively flat grade or slightly rolling topography. Steep slopes, heavy shade, compacted soils, lots of foot traffic, and poor air circulation should prompt you to consider alternatives. Resist the temptation to try to make do with grass on a poor site. The chart on p. 18 suggests solutions for several common problems.

Why Do Golf Courses Look So Good?

The best lawn in your neighborhood probably isn't a match for the local golf course. Homeowners often ask me why their yards don't look that good. I can offer a few reasons:

- **Time and effort.** The average homeowner spends two or three hours per week on the lawn, while maintaining a golf course is a full-time effort, not a weekend proposition.

- **Mowing height.** The closer a lawn is mowed, the denser and more attractive it becomes. The grass species used on putting greens tolerate very low mowing. The trouble is, once mowed this close, a lawn automatically becomes a high-maintenance item. In general, golf greens must be mowed daily, and few of us homeowners would relish that level of involvement.

- **Equipment.** Golf course superintendents use professional-grade equipment, such as reel mowers that cut the grass blades cleanly, like scissors, with very little abrasion to the plants. Most homeowners use rotary mowers, which cut the blades by beating them with a whirling hunk of steel, something like a hatchet.

- **Knowledge and training.** Golf course superintendents typically hold a degree in turfgrass management. Most homeowners rely on the information printed on packages of grass seed and fertilizer.

LAWN ALTERNATIVES

Problem	Possible Solution
Thin turf under shade trees	Plant shade-adapted ground covers or grasses.
High-traffic areas	Install bluestone, flagstone, or other pavers.
Moss or mildew in shady areas	Remove turf and moss, plant shade-adapted perennials, and add wood-chip mulch. Consider removing or pruning nearby trees to allow more sunlight penetration. Test the soil to determine if pH is a problem.
Grass on a steep slope	Plant junipers, Hall's honeysuckle, crown vetch, or other ornamentals on the slope.

Hell Strips

"Hell strip"? That's the ugly term for areas along sidewalks, surrounding your mailbox, and between driveways where the grass is stressed by the heat, salt, and compaction from foot traffic. Consider giving these trouble spots to short ornamental grasses and heat-tolerant perennials such as yarrow, junipers, fleeceflower, sedum, coreopsis, lilyturf, daylilies, and gazania.

A hell strip can be transformed into an attractive landscape feature by giving up on the grass and growing a low-maintenance perennial.

Choosing Your Maintenance Level

Once you decide where the grass is going to go, it's time to take a look at how you like to spend your weekends and then choose a maintenance level for the lawn. Not surprisingly, most folks want a high-maintenance look but are only willing to invest limited time and money. Try to be honest with yourself. Identify how many hours and dollars you—and your family—are willing to invest in a typical week, and base your design and planting decisions accordingly.

A *high-maintenance lawn* is generally mowed two or three times per week, receives 4 lb. or 5 lb. of nitrogen per 1,000 sq. ft. each year, and is regularly aerated and dethatched with power equipment. Applying nitrogen is key to encouraging turf growth, and high levels of nitrogen fertilizer make it necessary to mow more often. Pest control is given lots of attention, with regular inspections and both preventive and curative treatments. The lawn is watered whenever needed to keep the soil moist. In all, a high-maintenance lawn

will require an average of four or five hours a week. Kentucky bluegrass, creeping bentgrass, colonial bentgrass, improved bermudagrass, and dichondra are choices adapted to this high-input regimen. They will provide a beautiful emerald green color with a thick, luxurious appearance, and they are especially durable under hard use.

A *medium-maintenance lawn* receives the same type of care as one in a more ambitious program but at a reduced level. These lawns are mowed one or two times per week, receive 2 lb. to 3 lb. of nitrogen per year, and are aerated and dethatched as necessary. Pest control is provided on an as-needed basis, if and when problems arise. The lawn is watered to keep the soil moist, except when cutting back to save on utility bills or to conserve water. On the average, expect to spend two or three hours per week. This middle-of-the-road approach works well with Kentucky bluegrass, tall fescue, rough bluegrass, zoysia, bermuda, St. Augustine, and bahiagrass. The result should be a lawn that is green, healthy, and functional, with a moderate level of aesthetic appeal.

Just about everyone would like the look of a high-maintenance lawn. Not all of us care to devote the necessary time and expense, however, and easier alternatives can be nearly as attractive.

TURF TIP

Get a Referral

If you need help in planning your yard, ask friends for the names of landscape designers or architects. Call these professionals for a list of clients whose yards you might be able to visit. Even though you're only going to be referred to successful projects, you'll get a good idea of the designers' style.

A *low-maintenance lawn* is mowed two or three times per month, is treated with about 1 lb. of nitrogen per year, and receives soil aeration only if severe problems with drainage arise. In most cases, pest-control measures are nonexistent; if high levels of pests build up, you simply cross your fingers and hope that the grass will regrow and spread into the affected areas. On average, you'll invest just an hour or two per week. Choose from such cultivars as common, unimproved types of rough bluegrass, Kentucky bluegrass, tall fescue, bermuda, bahia, centipede, and buffalograss. Because these lawns require minimum amounts of time, cost, and effort, they are suited to a large property or to people who have little time or aptitude for yard work. Do you spend several weeks away from home each summer? Then go with a low-maintenance plan, unless you plan on hiring a lawn service.

You can follow a couple—or even all three—of these levels of lawn care. The very visible front yard might be high maintenance, the back medium, and the sides low. This approach gives you a presentable front lawn and a rugged backyard without unduly draining your leisure time.

Hiring a Landscape Pro

If you find that all of this staring at the yard is discouraging, then consider bringing in a professional to assist you. Don't feel embarrassed about asking for help. It's necessary to consider a multitude of factors in planning a lawn that will look good.

Whom should you call? You're probably used to getting free landscaping tips when buying seed and plants from a nursery or

Lawn Lingo

If you're going to do a good job of lawn care, it helps to be able to speak the language. Here are some of the most common terms:

- **Aeration.** Removing cores of soil and grass plants to introduce more oxygen, encourage the spread of roots, and improve drainage.

- **Compaction.** Compression of the soil to a degree that impedes root growth.

- **Cultivar.** A variety of a grass species.

- **Dormant period.** A time in which plants temporarily cease shoot and root growth, usually due to heat or cold. Dormant plants resume growth when conditions again become favorable.

- **Organic matter.** A nonmineral part of the soil, serving to supply and hold nutrients for the lawn and to help resist compaction.

- **Overseed.** To place seed in an existing lawn.

- **pH.** Refers to the alkalinity or acidity of soil or water. Low pH values (1.0 to 6.0) are acid, high values (8.0 to 14.0) are alkaline, and a pH of 7.0 is neutral.

- **Rhizome.** A grass stem growing horizontally under the soil surface.

- **Sod.** Plugs, squares, or strips of grass plants with adhering soil, used to start a lawn vegetatively rather than by seed.

- **Stolon.** A grass stem growing horizontally along the soil surface.

- **Thatch.** A layer of decomposing grassy material located between the grass blades and soil.

- **Winterkill.** Lawn injury that occurs during the winter dormant period.

garden center. Unfortunately, this isn't necessarily objective information—you may be encouraged to use stock of which the firm has an overabundance. An alternative is to pay for sound, unbiased advice. There are three groups of professionals that you can consult. Each performs many of the same tasks, yet specializes in certain areas.

Landscape architects

If you will be making major changes, such as adding a gazebo or putting up a retaining wall, you might want to contact a landscape architect. Safety is a concern with changes of this magnitude, and landscape architects are familiar with the loads that various materials and technologies can support. They will be able to spot unsafe or unstable features, such as steps that are too high and footings that would be insufficient for an arbor. Landscape architects must pass rigorous state testing to be licensed.

Landscape designers

Landscape designers focus more on the green side of the design. They can quickly draw good, flowing bed lines and identify the best locations for trees, shrubs, flowers, and lawn. They are especially valuable for selecting and locating plants in suitable places; landscape architects, on the other hand, may work with a smaller plant list, and they tend to have less experience in picking the best sites. The certification process is less demanding for designers but involves a measure of training beyond the basic skills of selecting plants at the nursery. It is wise to look for a certified landscape designer who is affiliated with the nurserymen's program in your state.

Gardening services

Ask your grandmother, and she'll probably remember making her own butter, soap, candles, and clothing. In recent years, it seems like you can hire almost anything to be done—even have someone walk your dog for you! The landscape is no different. Affectionately referred to as "Mow, Blow, and Go" guys, landscape crews offer a valuable service.

If you're always on the go, or if your idea of landscape enjoyment is *looking* at the yard rather than tending it, hire it done! The key to success with a gardener/landscape service is to remember that you're the boss: You should dictate which tasks (mowing, edging, fertilizing, pruning, mulching, etc.) should be done and how often the crew should show up.

Expect personalized assistance to cost several hundred dollars or more. Although the help should be well worth the expense, I suggest you take the time to begin with your own site inventory and analysis, then seek assistance as you need it.

A good landscape designer will match conditions of the site to the needs of the homeowner.

IT ALL BEGINS WITH SOIL

GOOD SOIL IS AS IMPORTANT TO YOUR LAWN as a good foundation is to your home. The grass plants need a fertile, porous growing medium if they are to perform well for you. That almost always means doing something to improve the soil that came with your property. Nevertheless, I find that homeowners tend to take soil for granted. "Out of sight, out of mind," their approach seems to be. After all, when you look out over the lawn, what do you see? Cheerful, green leaf blades. But they are only half of the picture, and this chapter deals with the all-important biological and chemical transactions that take place at the roots' level.

When it comes to roots, the bigger, the better—and soil quality is crucial if roots are to grow deep and wide. An extensive root system does a better job of picking up moisture and nutrients. It also serves to anchor the plant—not that a sprig of grass has the same trouble staying vertical as a sequoia, but you do want a stable footing for back-yard recreation. Your backyard volleyball games will be safer and more enjoyable if the players have firm footing.

Although soil seems pretty dense when you're trying to plant something in it, the good-quality stuff is about half solid matter (including minerals and organic substances) and half air space. Both are crucial to the performance of the lawn. The solid part provides nutrients and stability, while the empty part allows oxygen and water to reach the roots.

To put it plainly and simply, good soil is responsible for healthy landscapes.

It Isn't Just Dirt!

Soils vary in their proportion of three basic components—sand, clay, and silt—and a particular soil is often described in terms of its predominant ingredients. So it is that you'll come across the term "silty clay," for example. In its ideal combination, soil is known as loam, a mixture rich in organic matter and having a mineral balance of roughly 20 percent clay, 40 percent silt, and 40 percent sand. Loam does a good job of holding on to nutrients and water, while providing excellent drainage.

Organic matter is the end product of dead and decomposing plant leaves and litter. Your soil-test report should indicate a percentage of organic matter in the soil, usually between 0 percent and 5 percent; a good number is 3.5 percent to 4.5 percent, while a 1 percent content is too skimpy. Soil low in organic matter will not nourish the plants adequately or provide an appropriate habitat for beneficial microorganisms.

Sandy soils

Sandy soils are well drained, sometimes excessively so. The angular shape of those tiny particles creates a good deal of air space through which water passes quickly. In general, roots thrive in sandy soils. There is a good supply of oxygen, and the soil structure resists compaction—a particularly important point wherever there is a lot of foot traffic, such as along paths and adjacent to the patio or deck. Another plus is that these soils tend to discourage root-rot diseases.

The downside to a predominantly sandy soil is that it may not retain moisture well enough, requiring you to water frequently.

So, What's Your Soil Made Of?

After reading about all the things that go together to make good soil, you're probably wondering how your own yard rates. Here's a simple way to find out. Place 2 in. of soil into a large glass jar, add 6 in. of water, and put the lid back on. Shake vigorously for about 3 min., then allow the mixture to sit overnight.

The next day you'll see that the soil has settled out into visible layers. The sands are heaviest and make up the bottom layer. The silts are above that, then the clays. The uppermost component is a thin layer of organic matter.

Try this test on soils from various parts of the lawn, and while you're at it, take samples from the vegetable garden and flower beds for comparison. The findings can be revealing when it comes time to figure out what may be wrong with the lawn—or with the tomatoes and gaillardias.

Water

Organic matter

Clay

Silt

Sand

Sampling Errors

Be careful that fertilizers and amendments don't find their way into the soil samples you collect, or your test may be thrown off. Even a scattering of birdseed may make a test invalid.

You're also likely to make more passes with the fertilizer spreader because sand particles are slick and hard, much like marbles, and tend to allow nutrients to drain away. Take care to apply water and fertilizer in relatively light doses to compensate for the greater frequency.

Clay soils

Clay soils are made of extremely small particles arranged close together. The particles are flattened in shape and look something like tiny pancakes. When lawns growing on clay soils receive even moderate foot traffic, the particles are compacted, leaving little room for water and air. The tiny spaces that do remain will fill with water after a rainfall, displacing the oxygen essential for the root system. Because the water lodges in the soil rather than draining, roots stay wet and are prone to rot.

Clay soils have their advantages. They allow you to get by with watering and fertilizing less often. And by holding on to water and nutrients, they help prevent surface- and groundwater contamination from runoff.

Silty soils

Silt particles are smaller than those of sand and not much larger than clay particles. They perform much like clay soils, sticking together and tending to suffer from compaction. In some parts of the country, they are referred to as "muck" soils. Silty soils hold nutrients well, and most are naturally plentiful in soil nutrients, so that homeowners need to supply less fertilizer to the lawn.

Organic matter

Organic matter represents a relatively small part of most soils, but it plays a very important role, making the mineral structure "loamier," furnishing nutrients, and helping to hold on to water. Beneficial microorganisms take up housekeeping in the stuff, as well.

Testing Your Soil

Much as an IQ test (purportedly) measures a person's ability to learn, a soil test computes how well suited your yard is to growing a lush lawn. This simple diagnostic step will guide you in adjusting the soil's qualities to make it a better medium for grass. Test results can also help you identify grass cultivars that will perform best with your prevailing conditions; see chapter 7 for profiles of many lawn grasses. For a good-size yard, you may want to do a test for each of a few areas that show a different color and density. Refer back to the site inventory and site analysis described in chapter 1, as a reminder of any problems that should be investigated with a soil test.

You can buy a simple kit and do your own soil tests, or contact your local cooperative extension for advice on finding a test lab. To collect samples, arm yourself with a clean, dry plastic bucket (a metal bucket might interfere with the tests) and something to dig with. Take a handful of soil

RAISING pH WITH LIMESTONE

[1 LB. OF GROUND LIMESTONE PER 1,000 SQ. FT.]

Change in pH	Sandy Soil	Silty Soil	Clay Soil
4.5 to 6.5	50	160	200
5.0 to 6.5	40	130	150
5.5 to 6.5	30	90	100
6.0 to 6.5	15	50	55

To really get to know your lawn, you've got to get to know the soil, and a soil test is an excellent introduction. Take a few samples from around the yard and have them analyzed, either through a commercial lab or with a home kit.

from a depth of 2 in. or 3 in. Remove any thatch, roots, or grass blades from it—they cause inaccurate readings. You'll want five or ten samples from each lawn area you've identified, amounting to about a pint of soil. Mix the soil well in the bucket.

Most labs report their information in an easy-to-read chart format with recommendations on how much of a particular nutrient or amendment to add. If the pH is out of whack, you may also have to alter that so that the grass can take better advantage of the nutrients you're supplying.

If the reports shows that your soil is too acidic, you can bring that pH number up by adding ground limestone. If the soil is too alkaline, the most common remedy is spreading sulfur. It's best to add these amendments when first preparing a lawn— new homeowners have all the luck—but you can incorporate them with an established

LOWERING pH WITH SULFUR			
[1 LB. OF ELEMENTAL SULFUR PER 1,000 SQ. FT.]			
Change in pH	Sandy Soil	Silty Soil	Clay Soil
8.5 to 6.5	45	60	70
8.0 to 6.5	30	35	45
7.5 to 6.5	10	20	25
7.0 to 6.5	3	5	7

lawn by first aerating, then spreading the sulfur or limestone.

These materials are dusty, and although allergic reactions are not common, wear a dust mask when spreading them, as well as long pants and sleeves. Because a considerable dose of sulfur can burn the grass, apply it in measured doses over a period of months.

By spreading elemental sulfur over an alkaline soil, you can raise the soil's pH to a range that favors lawn grasses.

Common Problems

Few yards have ideal soils; most need some help. The best time to fix a problem is when starting a new lawn, but you can use gradual amendments if the lawn is already growing. Here are some of the situations that you might encounter and how to address them.

New lawns

As I drive past developments and look at the houses under construction, I shake my head at the sight of all that ravaged soil. These homeowners will end up paying thousands of dollars to build up their lawns, much of the money going to replace the good soil that has been lost in the process of grading the property.

In a natural, undisturbed setting, the top layer of soil is something known as duff.

This is a mixture of leaves and other plant parts that are in the process of being broken down by microorganisms. Below that is the topsoil, an excellent mixture of soil particles and the naturally composted organic matter known as humus; this soil layer receives nutrients as they wash down from the duff. Continuing down, we come to the subsoil, a less fertile layer that isn't as well suited for growing grass. Below that is the substratum, which can be described as rock on its slow, slow way to becoming soil-size particles. Finally, you reach a zone of bedrock, completely incapable of supporting a lawn. The relative depths of these layers varies tremendously from landscape to landscape (see the illustration on p. 30).

A lawn cannot be expected to thrive if there isn't a healthy layer of topsoil. Ideally, the topsoil should be scraped off and reserved in a pile, to be redistributed over the property after the construction and grading are completed. But often in new-home construction, the topsoil is trucked off and sold elsewhere. Or it is mixed indiscriminately with the other layers. The resulting disturbed layers will be less adequate than straight topsoil in meeting the needs of a new lawn. But all too often, the contractor is in a hurry to finish the job, and the homeowners are more concerned with unpacking moving cartons than making sure their dirt is in good shape. Only later does it become clear that a new lawn won't flourish on soil that is easily compacted, drains poorly, and has little fertility. The sad result is a very nice-looking home in the middle of a stunted landscape.

If you somehow missed out on the stockpile and redistribute approach, obtain a large quantity of compost, manure, or Canadian peat moss (these materials are rich in organic matter) and till them into the upper 4 in. to 6 in. of soil. Start out by spreading a couple of inches of materials over the whole site. On average, this will bring the organic-matter content up a percentage point or two, say from 1 percent to 3 percent.

Talk about getting off to a bad start—over half of all landscape problems that arise in the first five years are directly due to construction damage to the soil.

SOIL, GOOD AND BAD

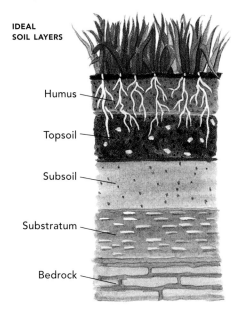

IDEAL
SOIL LAYERS

Humus

Topsoil

Subsoil

Substratum

Bedrock

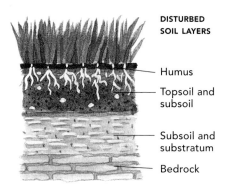

DISTURBED
SOIL LAYERS

Humus

Topsoil and
subsoil

Subsoil and
substratum

Bedrock

Top-Quality Topsoil

Like just about anything else you can buy for the home, the quality of topsoil varies widely. If you are buying a few truckloads to improve your soil, make sure the stuff really will be an improvement. It's a good idea to go to the source and have a close look at the soil before committing yourself.

Drainage, fast and slow

Both clay and sandy soils tend to have drainage problems but in different ways. Clay inhibits drainage, so you're apt to have standing water after a rain. Water percolates quickly through sandy soil, whisking away nutrients and causing the lawn to dry out.

The goal is to bring these soils closer to the loamy ideal. If you're starting from scratch, you have a chance to get good soil immediately. Aim toward incorporating 2 in. to 3 in. of compost if your soil contains a lot of clay or sand. If the soil could be called loamy already, then you might need no more than 1 in. of this life-supporting, leavening material. Spread the compost, then till it in thoroughly to a depth of 5 in. or 6 in.

Improving the soil's drainage doesn't have to be an all-or-nothing proposition in which you start with bare earth. You can also take smaller steps in the course of one or two growing seasons. Begin by going over the lawn with a core aerator, a power tool available at rental stores. Aerate the lawn twice in fall and twice in spring for northern lawns, and three to four times in summer for southern lawns. After each cultivation, add dried compost with a fertilizer spreader. See p. 33 for tips on distributing organic matter.

The quality of the soil isn't the only issue. The pitch of the lawn also can be a consideration. Water may not have time to seep into a steep slope, so that the grass there is chronically weakened by a lack of moisture. As the grass thins out, it tends to be less able to keep soil particles in place, and erosion results. You can avoid this problem by redesigning the landscape—installing a retaining wall, terracing the slope, or putting in a ground cover. Remember, grass is not the universal answer for every spot in the yard.

It may be that your lawn will remain stubbornly wet after all your work to fix the

COMMON MISTAKE

Sand for Soggy Soil

If your soil is heavy and doesn't drain well, you might be tempted to try adding sand to improve drainage. In fact, sand may combine with silt or clay particles to form a still more imperme-able layer. Instead, work in liberal amounts of compost.

The best time to increase the yard's organic content is before you put down a lawn; that way, peat moss or compost can be thoroughly worked into the upper layer of soil.

Grasses for Salty Soil

Whether the salt seeps into your lawn from the pavement or the seashore, try sowing the yard to bermudagrass, zoysia, or St. Augustinegrass for best results.

problem. An ambitious answer is to install a drainage system that collects water in perforated pipes and takes it away from the yard. The pipe is placed in a trench, resting on a bed of gravel to keep soil from clogging the system; then the lines are covered with more gravel. In places throughout the wet area, the gravel can be extended to the surface as catch basins for collecting water. Perforated covers are placed on the columns, flush with the ground, to keep soil out.

Soil, sweet and sour

Soil is referred to as "sweet" or "sour," depending on its relative alkalinity or acidity. Levels of acidity and alkalinity are described scientifically in terms of a pH number. Acid soils range from a pH of 1.0 to 6.9, and alkaline soils from 7.1 to 14.0. Neutral soils are given the designation 7.0. A soil with a pH of 5.0 is more acidic than one with a pH of 6.0; a pH of 8.3 is more alkaline than 7.5. In most of the eastern United States, soils are acidic. Midwestern and western soils tend to be neutral to alkaline.

Either low or high pH levels can lead to problems, the most serious of which is making nutrients less available—each nutrient has an optimal pH range. For nitrogen, there's a lot of latitude, from 5.5 to 9.0. Iron, on the other hand, is readily available only from 4.0 to 5.5. A plant can make use of a nutrient somewhat out of the ideal range but not at a level that will ensure good growth.

Generally, lawns grow best when the pH is slightly acidic, from 6.0 to 6.5. You can help to bring pH values into this range by modifying the soil with lime and by fertilizing. You can add fertilizer and lime at the same time; however, the best time to add either one in large quantities is before lawn establishment.

Too much salt is bad for lawns, just as it is for the people who tend them. Lawns are apt to get an overdose when nearby roadways are treated with salt to remove ice and snow. The grass will look pale, thin, and stunted. You can't do too much about the salt applied by the street crews, but when trying to keep your sidewalk and driveway clear, use calcium chloride instead of sodium chloride or potassium chloride; it burns the turf less. Better yet, use a 50/50 mixture of calcium chloride and sand to provide some melting action as well as traction for passersby.

Affordable Amendments

Compost, sulfur, and ground limestone are the ingredients most often used to improve the soil. Knowing what to add is one thing; knowing where to get it inexpensively is quite another.

You'll need more compost than you can generate with yard trimmings and kitchen waste. Check with local recycling centers to see if they give away or sell compost. Or, ask friends who are members of gardening clubs about their sources. These folks tend to be fanatical about improving the soil in their gardens.

For large quantities of sulfur or limestone, contact builders or landscape design/build firms and ask if they will allow you to "pool buy" with them on their next purchase. An order of this size will have a much lower unit cost than you could find at a garden or home center.

Nutrient overload or deficiency

Lawns that are overloaded with nutrients can look just as bad as those damaged by wintertime applications of salt. The underlying cause may be similar, in fact. Many synthetic lawn fertilizers are salt based, so when you lay on too much of these fertilizers, the lawn gets an overload of salt as well. Extra nutrients tend to be more of a problem with clay soils, as they hold nutrients quite well.

Just as too much nutrition is bad, so is not enough. Lawns growing on nutrient-poor soils, or those that are maintained at a very low fertility level, tend to be thin, weak, and subject to weed invasion. These problems can be detected with a simple soil fertility test and fixed by adding a fertilizer that supplies what the soil is lacking.

Not enough organic matter

Lawns are often deficient in organic matter, either because the soil was initially poor or because it was devalued in the construction process. The content will gradually improve with the age of a lawn, if clippings are returned to it, but this is a very slow process—even a 30-year-old lawn may not have enough to achieve the best results.

Ideally, your soil will have from 3 percent to 5 percent organic matter—a loamy mixture. If so, it will benefit from a modest 1-in. layer of compost. A reading of 1 percent or less means that you should work in 3 in. to 4 in. For a new lawn, spread the compost and then till it in. For an established lawn, apply the compost gradually, a few times each year. Prepare the lawn by going over it

To incorporate organic matter with an existing lawn, first aerate it, then scatter dry compost. In time, the compost will work down into the lawn.

with an aerator, then put down just enough compost to fill the holes left by the process.

Use either a drop or rotary spreader, opening the gate wide enough to allow the compost to flow through. Dry compost is much easier to work with, and its particle size should be somewhat uniform; otherwise, the spreader is apt to clog and apply the compost unevenly. To help move the compost off the grass blades and into the holes left by the aerator, you can drag the lawn with a piece of chain-link fence or go over it with a stiff rake.

TURF TIP

Giving Up on Grass

Need a ground cover that's tougher than grass, to withstand the daily abuse of kids and dogs? Sorry, but there isn't one. Grass is your most rugged alternative, and if it can't stand up to the traffic, you have to either live with the bare spots or redirect the traffic.

STARTING THE LAWN

HAVE FOUND THAT IF I SIMPLY SLAP SOME PAINT on my house without bothering with the prep work, I'll soon be disappointed with the results. The paint starts to peel, and my quick fix turns out to be a waste of time and money. You're apt to get the same results when starting a new lawn if you skip the preliminary steps and go straight to scattering seed. Your options for what to plant are varied. Seed, sod, plugs, and sprigs all work. Your decision will

be based on expense, size of your lawn, and how fast you want a finished lawn. Of course, all of these methods can also be used to fill in bare spots or repair bad patches in your existing lawn.

The First Steps

Once the backhoe and grading equipment have gone, it's time to look over your yard for construction debris that might be lurking at or just below the soil surface. Hunks of

concrete, pieces of drywall, paint buckets, and small pieces of wood—these are the leftovers that are apt to litter the site. I find that it helps to probe the area with a sharpened length of rebar or a cutoff golf club.

Weeds are likely to appear right around the time the builder hands you the keys to your new home or addition. Nutsedge, dandelions, clover, prostrate knotweed, and field bindweed are a few of the typical culprits.

For best results, remove weeds from the lawn area by applying a nonselective herbi-

**CHECKING PERCENT GRADE WITH
A LINE LEVEL**

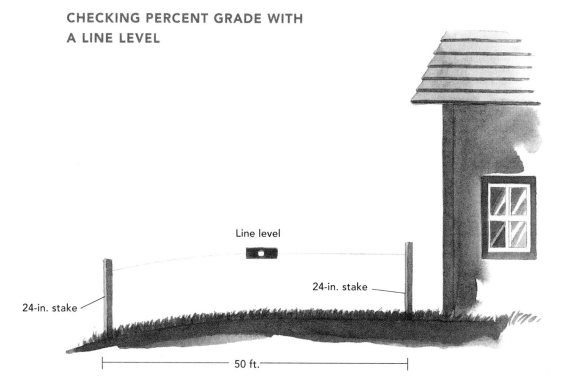

Line level

24-in. stake

24-in. stake

50 ft.

cide such as Roundup® or Finale®. These products are popular choices because they kill the roots as well as the shoots of a variety of weeds without leaving a residue in the soil to prevent the growth of the new grass plants. You can weed the yard by hand, of course, but this is a lot of work, and if you don't get the roots up, the plants probably will grow back. (For more on weeds, see chapter 6.)

Keep up your grades

After the weeds are removed, rough-grade the lawn area by raking to smooth out the high and low spots. Within 100 ft. of the house, use a line level to make sure that there is a 2 percent to 3 percent slope away from the foundation. A line level is a small tube of liquid in which a bubble is visible through a window, similar to the levels used in carpentry; you can buy them at home centers and hardware stores. Real estate agents, house inspectors, and contractors have told me about their nightmarish experiences with foundation failures and wet basements that resulted from a grade pitching toward the house.

To use a line level, pound a 24-in.-long stake into the ground near the foundation and another stake 50 ft. out in the yard. Run a taut string between them, with the end at the house touching the ground. Attach the line level to the string and read the bubble in the liquid (see the illustration on the facing page). If the bubble is on the side of the level *toward* the house, the ground slopes away as it should. If it's on the side *away* from the

Coping with Slopes

If part of your yard is on a steep grade, consider an alternative to the usual method of seeding. Installing sod will work, if you peg the pieces to keep them from slipping. Or you can turn that slope into a series of flat areas by terracing; you may want a landscape architect's help in constructing a terrace that will both prevent erosion and fit in with the overall theme of the landscape.

Hydroseeding, routinely used on hillsides along public highways, can be an answer to a precipitous home lawn. A slurry of ground wood cellulose, seed, and starter fertilizer is sprayed over the slope. The cellulose acts as a mulch to help the seed stay in place long enough to germinate. Hydroseeding is expensive—and definitely not a do-it-yourself project—so consider it only for large-scale areas where there are no other options.

house, water may be headed for your foundation; consider calling the contractor about regrading the site.

To make sure the pitch away from the house is adequate, have a helper lift the downhill stake until the line level reads in the middle. Measure the height the stake has been raised. An elevation of 1 ft., for a 50-ft. string, means the pitch is 2 percent. Repeat these steps out another 50 ft. from the house. An overall pitch of less than 2 percent may be cause for concern.

While you've got the tape measure out, calculate the approximate area of the new lawn so that you'll know how much fertilizer, seed, and pest control agents to purchase. Most products are applied in terms of a certain quantity per 1,000 sq. ft. of lawn.

TURF TIP

Develop an Eye for Area

It's not difficult to estimate lawn areas by eye. Start off by measuring a 25-ft. by 40-ft. rectangle and putting a stake or flag in each corner. This is 1,000 sq. ft. Get a feel for just how big that is, then mentally transpose it around the yard to come up with a rough total of the area.

Building up the bare soil

One good thing about all the trouble of starting a new lawn is that this is the best opportunity you'll ever have to incorporate organic matter, fertilizer, and other amendments. To find out just what your yard needs to bring it up to snuff, see chapter 2 for information on improving the soil.

Just before you are ready to plant, do a final grading to prepare a smooth planting surface. It's much easier to do this with a golf-course superintendent's bunker rake than with the common garden rakes available at hardware stores. This professional tool is about twice as wide as a garden rake and yet weighs no more; contact a local golf-course superintendent for a source. An alternative is to use a 3-ft. to 4-ft. section of chain-link fence, tying a rope to the corners and dragging it behind you to remove stones and to smooth out rough spots. Note the particle size of the soil as you grade; stop working when it is roughly pea size, rather than reducing it to a fine powder. When you are finished, use the line and level again to make sure that the grade is still at least 2 percent away from the house.

Seeding

As I've mentioned, the success of a new lawn depends on the time and effort given to soil preparation (see chapter 2). Much of this work is hard and sweaty, and you'll find that seeding is fun and easy in comparison. The only real trick is to pick the right grass. (Chapter 7 is devoted to the pros and cons of each grass species.)

When you shop for seed, have a look at the packaging label. It should list the percentages of each component. *Crop seed* can be deceiving because it sounds like a good thing but usually includes grass species you wouldn't want on your lawn—brome, timo-

Lawns for Active Kids

Backyard baseball games, roughhousing, and hide-and-seek are tough on a lawn. Prepare with a wear-resistant grass species that tolerates foot traffic.

In the South, zoysia and bermudagrass are the best options. Zoysia is a bit more durable but somewhat slower to recover from injury; other than that, there's no clear advantage between the two, so go by appearance and shade tolerance when making a choice. St. Augustine and centipede are warm-season species that rate poorly in terms of wear resistance, while bahiagrass is intermediate.

In the North, tall fescue and perennial ryegrass can help deal with high traffic. Both are initially wear tolerant but have no ability to grow back after damage has occurred. Fortunately, they are the two fastest-germinating cultivars and can be re-established quickly by sowing seed in bare patches.

No matter which grass you decide on, heavy use may mean annual renovation, including aeration, power-raking, replanting, watering, and fertilizing, as described in chapter 5.

Get it out while you can. You have only one chance to remove rocks, brick, plaster, boards, and other debris; seize the opportunity before planting.

thy, and perhaps bentgrass. If a mixture has as little as 1 percent to 2 percent crop seed, your lawn soon could be filled with undesirable plants. *Inert matter* is not necessarily a bad ingredient and simply represents whatever will not grow, such as stems and seed coverings that weren't removed in processing. The *weed seed* percentage should be as low as possible, of course, preferably well below 1 percent. Check the *germination rate*; seed with a rate lower than 90 is a poor buy.

Seeding is pretty simple, if you have a spreader and a kitchen scale. (Hand seeding is fine for small areas or repair jobs but not a whole lawn.) Following the directions on the seed package, weigh out the seed required for 1,000 sq. ft., then divide it into two batches. (The amount required varies with

Plan Your Water System

Before you plant is your best chance to install an underground sprinkler system. It's certainly not required in order to have a high-quality lawn—there are many good lawns that lack them. But you'll find that a system is a real time-saver; this will be especially welcome if dragging around sprinkler hoses isn't your idea of a leisure activity. About half the cost of a system is in the labor of putting pipes and valves in the ground, so if you're handy with basic plumbing tools, consider doing the job yourself. There may be potential maintenance tasks as well. Some systems require that all water be removed or "blown out" before winter to avoid having the pipes break from freezing. And from time to time, parts such as heads and valves have to be replaced.

TURF TIP

No Old Seed

You shouldn't have to worry about old seed. Grass will not grow well from seed that's more than a year old, and stores are strongly encouraged to discard old stock—but check the date on the label to make sure.

each species; for Kentucky bluegrass, you'll need about 3 lb., so each batch will be 1½ lb.) Apply the first half in a single back-and-forth direction, setting the spreader so that you cover the area thinly but evenly, making sure there is a little overlap with each pass. If a considerable amount of seed is left over after this first pass, you haven't put it on heavy enough. Or, if you run out of seed before you're done, you're putting on too much. In either case, make an adjustment in the application rate.

After applying the seed, go over it *lightly* with a rake to ensure good seed-to-soil contact; don't use a stiff-tine rake because it tends

WHAT YOU'LL NEED

Seeding
- ✓ Kitchen scale
- ✓ Spreader
- ✓ Roller
- ✓ String and stakes
- ✓ Lawn sprinkler or irrigation system
- ✓ Seed

to dig in too deeply. It's best to place the seed at a depth of about 2 times to 2½ times its width, which means less than ⅛ in.

Once the seed is in place, consider whether to roll the area. Rolling improves the contact between seed and soil and also evens out any undulations that developed while seeding. The downside to rolling is that it can compact the soil, especially if it is high in clay or silt; you may want to use the roller without any water in the drum. Sandy, loamy soil will benefit without suffering from compaction, and you can add water to the drum so that the roller will work harder for you. Start with it roughly a quarter full—that may be all the weight you need.

Pregerminate for a Prompt Lawn

You may want to try pregerminating to reduce your lawn's germination time once it's planted. It's an easy way to get a green lawn faster. Fill a couple of fine-mesh bags (or old panty hose) with lawn seed, soak them in a 5-gal. bucket of water for 24 hr., then hang them from the clothesline to drain. After a few hours, dump the seed into a wheelbarrow and stir with a trowel to dry so that it will flow through a spreader for sowing. This method is particularly effective with Kentucky bluegrass, reducing germination time from 22 days to 12 days.

TOOL TALK SHOPPING FOR A SPREADER

A *DROP SPREADER* IS THE BEST choice for seeding. Below the seed hopper is a metering device that drops seed directly onto the soil. A *rotary spreader* broadcasts over a wide area, using the centrifugal action of an impeller. This allows you to quickly plant a large area, but coverage tends to be somewhat uneven because grass seed is very light and prone to drifting in even the mildest of breezes. And the time saved is not significant—seeding a 5,000-sq.-ft. lawn with a drop spreader takes only about 15 min.

A rotary spreader comes into its own when applying fertilizer, so you may want to buy both models; you can split the purchase price with a neighbor or simply rent a spreader as needed.

COMMON MISTAKE

Buying Bargain Seed

Resist the temptation to save money by shopping for inexpensive seed. If you see a store display with several metal garbage cans of seed marked at a very low price, keep on walking.

To ensure that grass seed will have good contact with the soil, go over the newly seeded lawn lightly with a rake.

TWO-STEP SEEDING AND SPREADING

ROLLING A NEWLY SEEDED LAWN

Getting the lawn off to a good start

Start watering immediately after the seed is in place. If you had an underground sprinkler system installed, this is a simple and easy chore. If not, you will be facing several days of moving hoses around and tromping through mud and on top of new grass

SHOPPING FOR SEED

Kentucky bluegrass	2.0–3.0 lb./1,000 sq. ft.
Perennial ryegrass	3.0–4.0 lb./1,000 sq. ft.
Fine fescue	3.0–4.0 lb./1,000 sq. ft.
Tall fescue	9.0–10.0 lb./1,000 sq. ft.

plants. Try your best to keep the soil moist but not soggy. As is always the goal, no matter how mature the lawn, water the entire depth of the root zone. With new grass plants, this isn't very deep—about 1 in. You can check the soil moisture in the top 1 in. of soil simply by sticking your finger into the newly seeded area—it should feel moist, not dry or soggy. Ideally, water for just a few minutes at a time but two times or three times per day.

Should you spread straw? A familiar suburban sight is a light covering of straw over a new lawn. Is straw worth the bother?

If you are establishing new grass on a slope or in a windy area, straw will help to hold the seed in place and slow the drying of the soil. It takes about 10 bales to handle 1,000 sq. ft. if you spread the straw so that the stems are only one or two layers thick— just enough to cover the seed and provide some moisture retention without encouraging the straw or seed to rot. You can purchase straw from farm-supply stores and local farms. Bales of hay will also do the job, but they are more expensive and often introduce unwanted seeds to the new lawn.

There are a few drawbacks to using straw. Wheat straw can introduce its own seed, so you may end up with a scattering of wheat plants in the midst of the lawn. Seeds from oat straw also may germinate, but unlike wheat the plants will not live through the winter to become persistent weeds. Straw can be a mess, too. It blows all over the place, and you'll probably track it into your house. Finally, the added expense of straw can be significant for a large area. If you are careful to water often enough to keep the soil from drying out, you may be able to skip the straw altogether.

Whether or not you go with straw, once the lawn is up and growing you should add nutrients in order to encourage the growth of the root system. When you see about 1½ in. to 2 in. of growth, apply a phosphorus-rich starter fertilizer with a ratio of nitrogen, phosphorus, and potassium of around 9-24-3. You'll find this product alongside the regular fertilizers in hardware stores and garden centers. The extra amount of phosphorus ensures that the young plants will be able to draw enough of this nutrient out of the soil. One application will suffice, as most soils have a relatively adequate level of phosphorus; apply too much and the grass can become soft and vulnerable to various diseases.

Sodding

When establishing a lawn with pieces of commercially grown sod, the ground preparation should be exactly the same as for seeding. Even though the sod comes with soil attached to it, soil prep still matters. One important difference is that the final grade should be about ¾ in. lower than for seeding, to allow for the thickness of the sod when approaching walks and patios.

Sod is expensive, and doing a whole lawn can be cost prohibitive—but you do get instant gratification. But don't forget you can use sod to fill in bare spots or to repair a bad patch, which won't be too expensive and will fill in fast.

Buying and choosing sod

If you're in good health and don't have a bad back, you can save some money by sodding the lawn yourself. Buy the sod from a garden center, or contact sod installers to see if they will sell stock to you. Some states require that sod be certified by the department of agriculture. Make sure that you buy inspected, certified sod comprised of cultivars

---

TURF TIP

Self-Sealing Sod

The easiest way to deal with any gaps between pieces of sod is to fill them with topsoil and allow the new lawn's rhizomes to conceal the bare areas.

When laying down a sod lawn, make sure you don't intermix rolls from different lots in a conspicuous part of the yard.

WHAT YOU'LL NEED

Sodding
- ✓ Sturdy knife to cut sod
- ✓ Wheelbarrow to transport sod
- ✓ Trowel
- ✓ Roller
- ✓ String and stakes
- ✓ Lawn sprinkler or irrigation system
- ✓ Sod

recommended by the land-grant university in your state or approved for your state by the National Turfgrass Evaluation Program (NTEP). For assistance, contact your county extension agent. Chapter 7 discusses selecting a suitable cultivar from the hundreds that are available.

If you're planning to establish an entire lawn, then it's wise to place an order several weeks in advance so the sod can be cut from a single lot; otherwise, you may get pieces from more than one lot, resulting in an inconsistent look. This is no big deal if you can use one lot of sod for the backyard and another for the front and sides, but a switch of lots in the middle of the yard will eventually show up as a noticeable difference in color, texture, and stiffness.

To order sod, measure each lawn area carefully, then calculate the square footage. The standard roll of sod covers an area of 6 sq. ft. For every 1,000 sq. ft. of lawn, you'd need a minimum of 167 rolls of sod, but be sure to order extra to replace pieces that don't establish themselves. To avoid the awkward problem of having a shift in color or growth habit in the middle of the lawn, tell the supplier you want sod taken from only one field.

The sod will arrive in rolled or folded strips, usually about 1½ ft. by 4 ft. (You also can hire installers to truck in big rolls of sod,

Commercially grown sod is a living carpet, one that will send its roots down into your prepared soil. Sodding is the fastest way to establish a mature lawn.

4 ft. or 5 ft. wide by perhaps 15 ft. long, for a speedy installation with fewer gaps; this approach is suited to larger lawns without many obstructions.) Unstack and unroll the sod as soon as possible after it is delivered to the site, inspecting the strips as you unload them. They should be moist and have a fresh, dark green color; otherwise, you've got an inferior lot and shouldn't have to pay for it. If you're going to be delayed for a day or two, lay the unrolled pieces on a hard-surface area out of the sun, such as a garage, carport, or shaded patio. Sprinkle with water to keep them from drying out.

Water the lawn area daily to prepare it for sodding, but stop the day before installation so that the surface will be firm enough to keep the installer from sinking into the soil.

Carpeting the yard

Start the installation along a straight edge in the landscape, such as a sidewalk or drive-way. Place the pieces of sod close together without overlapping, and avoid stretching them to fit, so that they'll be less likely to shrink noticeably. If the weather is hot, install the sod in sections of no more than 1,000 sq. ft., water the sod for 15 min. or so, then install another section and water it.

Arrange the pieces in a bricklike pattern, staggering the joints between the rows of sod. Cut the pieces to fit around light poles and irregularly shaped patio pavers. Try not to fill gaps narrower than 3 in. or 4 in. with a piece of sod; these small pieces tend to dry out, leaving the lawn with unsightly patches. Instead, fill them in with good soil and allow the sod squares to knit themselves. If you're installing tall fescue sod, sprinkle tall fescue seed over the soil to speed things along. You

may have to use pegs or tent stakes on slopes to keep the sod from slipping or unrolling.

After the sod is in place and watered, it can be rolled to make sure the new lawn fits tightly and that the roots are in good contact with the soil. In regions that are prone to compaction—most of the country qualifies—less pressure is called for, so the roller can be empty or only partially filled.

Sections of sod are laid down as you would stack bricks, offsetting the joints between squares.

Comparing Seed and Sod

Seed or sod? The most important considerations are price, haste, and timing. If you're in a big hurry to have an established lawn, then sod may be your answer. If you are on a tight budget, then be patient and seed your lawn; the cost of sod will run 10 to 20 times that of seeding, and this doesn't include the considerable expense of installing the sod.

As for timing, sod can be put down just about whenever the soil is not frozen because it already has a few roots and enough thatch to hold moisture for them. When seeding, however, you should try to do it under ideal conditions—warm (but not hot) weather with periods of gentle rain.

Sod tends to shrink as it dries, and you may want to overseed the bare areas that appear between the pieces. For a uniform appearance, make sure that you seed with the same cultivar (or mix of cultivars) used by the sod company.

The newly sodded lawn should be protected from foot traffic for at least a month, using string, bright flags, and stakes. Apply starter fertilizer to the new sod about a week or so after it is installed, following the directions on the product label. Get out the mower once the grass is fairly tall and the

sod has anchored itself to the soil, and set the mower somewhat higher than usual. Delay broadleaf-herbicide application for several weeks in order to allow the grass to become well established. Water the new sod daily, with just enough volume to keep it and the top inch of soil under it moist.

Plugging and Sprigging

You can think of the idea of starting a lawn with plugs and sprigs as establishing many little colonies of grass plants. The lawn gets off to a rapid start, relative to waiting for seed to germinate and grow into something more than a thin fuzz. Sodding remains the only means of having the near-instant gratification of an established lawn, but it costs more than plugging and sprigging. Another advantage is that these pieces of turf can be used over a longer part of the year than grass seed; depending on your region and the weather, you may be able to plug or sprig from April through June and again when things cool down, from September into

TOOL TALK **BLADE ROLLING**

LAWN ROLLERS are a traditional implement for getting a yard off to a good start, no matter what method you use to establish it—seed, sod, plugs, or sprigs. That even pressure helps the seed or new plants to come in contact with the life-giving soil. But this doesn't mean you have to use one—or even should use one. That weight may make heavy soils heavier still.

A roller is simply a metal drum in which you can put water to apply more pressure. For easily compacted soils, you may choose to not add any water. Otherwise, use the drum only one-quarter to one-half full. You can gauge the level of water by lowering a stick into the drum.

This isn't a tool you'll be using often, so it makes sense to borrow one from a neighbor or pick one up at a rental agency.

November. You'll see the best results if you get to work in late spring.

Plugs and sprigs are the usual means of starting some grasses, certain warm-season varieties in particular. These varieties either don't produce fertile seed or fail to grow true to seed; this means they can be reproduced only vegetatively, with clumps of the plants themselves.

Consider using sprigs and plugs as a fairly quick means of repairing a lawn with bare patches. The green will come back faster than if you were to scratch the surface and sprinkle seed.

Plugs

Plugs are little clumps of sod, about 2 in. square, that are planted in a pattern over the lawn area. Buffalograss, zoysiagrass, and bermudagrass are commonly established by this method. Plugs are available in garden centers in warmer areas of the country and can also be purchased through mail-order companies. Or, you can buy regular pieces of sod from a contractor or garden center and cut them into plugs yourself. Consistency counts when plugging a lawn, if you are to avoid having areas that differ in color or growth habit. Be sure to use the same cultivar throughout the lawn, rather than switching midway through in order to take advantage of a bargain. If you are plugging to repair a lawn, try to use the cultivar that makes up the principal part of the existing grasses.

Make sure that plugs are kept moist if there will be a delay before setting them into the lawn. They have a somewhat shorter shelf life than sod because the pieces are smaller and more vulnerable to drying. Lightly sprinkle them with water and store in a shaded place.

SHOPPING FOR SPRIGS AND PLUGS	
[FROM 55 SQ. FT. OF SOD]	
Bermudagrass	1 bushel of sprigs or 2-in. plugs on 6-in. spacing in rows 6 in. apart.
Zoysiagrass	1 bushel of 2-in. plugs on 6-in. spacing in rows 6 in. apart.

Plant the plugs in a grid pattern. Space them according to your budget—the closer you plant them, the faster they will develop into a lawn but the more the lawn will cost. An 18-in. spacing between plugs will usually take 50 percent longer to become established than a 12-in. spacing. Of course each grass species has a different rate of establishment, but you can expect a lawn with the wider spacing to take 12 weeks or more to fully grow in.

If you space the plugs 12 in. apart, you'll need about 1,000 of them to establish an area of 1,000 sq. ft. With a spacing of just 6 in., you'll need 4,000. As with sodding, be sure to purchase enough to complete the job.

PLUGS

Lawn Repair
When using seed, plugs, or sprigs to rescue a dead area of lawn, there's no need to remove all the dead grass. Just rake the affected area so that some bare ground shows through the browned blades, then seed, plug, or sprig. The canopy of dead grass will help protect the new plants from drying.

WHAT YOU'LL NEED

Plugging
- ✓ Plugger or bulb planter
- ✓ Rake
- ✓ String and stakes
- ✓ Lawn sprinkler or irrigation system
- ✓ Plugs

It is common for a few plugs to die, so buy 5 percent to 10 percent extra for replanting.

To plant each plug, remove a core of soil using either a specialty tool called a plugger or a long-handled bulb planter. Carefully place the plugs in the holes. They should establish themselves quickly through the horizontal expansion of their stolons and rhizomes, especially if the soil has been properly prepared, as for seeding and sodding. To help the plugs get on their way, go over the new lawn with a roller, as for sodding.

After planting, it's crucial to keep the soil moist; you can water longer and less frequently than with grass seed because the plug roots go deeper in the ground and benefit from a soaking. Fertilize once, at one-half to one-third the usual recommended rate. All those empty spaces between little plants are an invitation to weeds. Go after them with a hoe until the plugs have been growing a month or two, then consider applying an herbicide. After about six weeks, mow the new lawn to help encourage the plants to spread.

Sprigs

Sprigs are sections of grass plants that include a short piece of stolon or rhizome and roots and leaves, but no soil. Sprigging is often used to start lawns of St. Augustine, bermuda, and zoysia. This method is less expensive than plugging and may give a

LONG-HANDLED BULB PLANTER

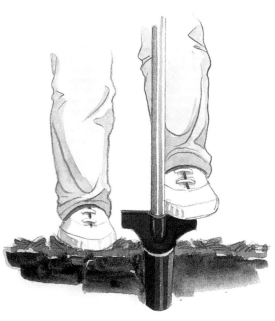

A new lawn can be established quickly by tucking plugs into the ground.

faster rate of cover. But sprigs usually require more care than plugs and aren't as hardy. Sprigs are commonly sold by the bushel, and on average it takes 3 bushels to 5 bushels to establish 1,000 sq. ft. They can be purchased in spring or summer from garden centers. As with plugs, you have the option of buying sod and cutting or pulling it apart into single sprigs.

Sprigs can be established on a grid pattern, with spacing similar to that used for plugs but less precise; use a stick to press each sprig into the soil. They can also be planted in rows, something like tiny row-crop vegetables. Use a hoe or hand cultivator to cut a shallow (2-in. to 3-in.) furrow into the prepared soil, and place the sprigs 6 in. to 9 in. apart. Press the soil around them. Go over the lawn with a roller, as for sodding.

Because there's not much mass to keep the plants from drying out, start watering the area as soon as possible, and be sure to keep it moist until the lawn is well underway. Administer one dose of fertilizer, at one-half to one-third the usual recommended rate. As with plugs, control weeds by nimbly nicking them with a hoe; you can switch to an herbicide after a month or two. Give the sprigged lawn its first mowing at six weeks or so.

SPRIG

PLANTING SPRIGS

If Your Lawn Won't Grow

Unfortunately, lots of things can go wrong when establishing a lawn. I'll go over the four most common problems here and suggest remedies for each.

Poor germination

If the new lawn is thin, then poor germination is probably the cause. This is apt to

occur in one of a few ways. First, if a mixture of grasses was used, you may have stopped watering the new lawn after only the fastest-growing cultivar emerged, leaving the others with insufficient moisture. Each component of a mix requires a certain time for germination. The classic combination includes Kentucky bluegrass, requiring 20 days to germinate, and perennial ryegrass, taking only about half as long. Homeowners

simple act of mowing. If a few weeds persist, you can nail them with a postemergence broadleaf herbicide such as Trimec® or Weed-B-Gon®. Grassy types of weed can be pulled by hand or spot-treated with Roundup or Finale. Wait until the lawn has been mowed a few times, and the grass has had a chance to establish good root structure, before applying an herbicide.

If you have a low tolerance for grassy weeds, consider applying Siduron (sometimes sold as Tupersan®) after seeding. This pre-emergence herbicide has the unusual quality of preventing crabgrass from germinating while allowing the desirable grasses to grow. Siduron is quite expensive (about two times to three times the cost of a typical pre-emergence product) and only prevents 60 percent to 70 percent of the crabgrass from germinating, but it may be worth a try if you've had trouble with crabgrass in previous years.

Weeds are apt to give the new grass plants more competition than they can handle. You can spray with a pre-emergence herbicide or be ruthless with your weeding.

tend to make the mistake of faithfully watering until the ryegrass appears, then greatly cutting back so that the bluegrass fails to emerge. Make sure that you water until all of the species or cultivars in the mix have time to germinate.

Another cause of poor germination is simply too little water. You may have to adjust your watering schedule to compensate for the drying effects of wind and temperature. Finally, there is the quality of the seed itself. Cheap seed usually has poor germination. The expense of seed is the least costly part of a lawn, so buy a premium product for the best long-term results.

Weeds

It's not at all uncommon to see at least a few weeds in a newly seeded lawn. The good news is that most will be controlled by the

Uneven or sunken areas

If a newly graded yard has pockets of lightweight soil, these products may sink below the rest of the lawn. The best remedy for this isn't an easy fix. Dig out the entire sunken area to a depth of at least 18 in. and fill it with a soil mix that comes as close as possible to the surrounding soil. Using lightweight topsoil or compost will only result in another soil collapse. Using a section of 4-in. by 4-in. post, lightly tamp the soil as you fill the hole, adding about 4 in. at a time until this area is roughly 2 in. higher than the soil around it. In time, the slight crown should settle to approximately the same level as the rest of the lawn.

Gaps in the sod

As the strips of sod dry somewhat and contract, you're apt to see gaps around the edges. Fill in the spaces with topsoil, and wait for the grass to spread. Potting soil is a better (but costly) alternative because it won't introduce weed seeds to your new lawn.

Follow-Up Care

Postplanting attention is vital for a new lawn if it is to thrive. Take the time to cordon off the area with stakes and string. Then plan on tending to the lawn, daily at first, seeing that its need for moisture is met.

After the first three weeks, a newly seeded lawn changes from a fragile work in progress to a more rugged, semiestablished planting.

Consult the chart "Day Care for Young Lawns" below. For the next three weeks, continue to care for the lawn as outlined for Week Three, watching for changes in thickness and rooting of the grass plants. If all goes well, seeded lawns usually need eight weeks to ten weeks to become established, then they are ready for the regular maintenance procedures outlined in chapters 4 and 5. You can consider a sodded lawn to be mature after six weeks. For sprigs and plugs, the more intensively you've planted these bits of life, the quicker the lawn will be rugged enough for romping. At best, you'll get good coverage within six weeks, but you may not have a full-fledged lawn for a couple of months.

TURF TIP

The Maiden Mowing

Take it easy the first time out with the mower. The new lawn will be easily rutted, so mow on a day when the soil is relatively dry.

DAY CARE FOR YOUNG LAWNS

	Week One	Week Two	Week Three
SODDED LAWNS	Water enough each day to keep the upper 1 in. to 2 in. of soil moist. Keep people off the new lawn.	Water every day, or every other day, to keep the upper 3 in. of soil moist. Keep foot traffic to a minimum. Apply a starter fertilizer to encourage root growth. Gently lift a corner of a sod piece to check for root growth into the soil.	Water to keep the upper 6 in. of soil moist. Keep foot traffic to a minimum. Begin mowing.
SEEDED AND PLUGGED LAWNS	Water several times each day to keep the upper 1 in. to 2 in. of soil moist. Keep people off the new lawn.	Water several times each day to keep the upper 4 in. of soil moist. Apply starter fertilizer. Look for germination differences between varieties; remember to keep watering until all grasses germinate.	Water to keep the upper 6 in. of soil moist. Keep foot traffic to a minimum. Begin mowing when the new grass reaches 3 in. tall.

CHAPTER 4

Mowing 101

A Fertilizing Primer

Watering Wisdom

MOWING, FERTILIZING, AND WATERING

THE ROUTINE TASKS OF KEEPING THE LAWN SHORN, FED, AND WATERED make all the difference between a so-so lawn and one that is a pleasure to maintain—and gaze upon. Mowing is the most basic of all lawn-care operations, as I'm sure I don't have to remind you. Most folks think of it as nothing but a chore, when in fact mowing offers a regular opportunity to nudge up the quality of your lawn a couple of notches. Fertilizing has even less appeal for most

homeowners—you don't get that pleasant scent of fresh-mown grass, and the results aren't immediately visible. You may be tempted to get by without spreading on a balanced diet of nutrients. But you'll never see a farmer who doesn't go over the fields with regular applications of fertilizer, and a lawn is no different. As for water, there are times when nature provides all a lawn needs—and more. In most parts of the

country, however, the rains have to be supplemented with watering if lawns are to look lush.

Chances are none of this is news to you. But you may not know that mowing, fertilizing, and watering can help prevent diseases, pest infestations, and weed outbreaks. If you think of these tasks as preventative, you may have more energy to go out there and tend to them as needed.

Mowing is more than a means of keeping the lawn from looking shaggy. If done conscientiously, it will make the grass plants greener and more resilient.

Mowing 101

Mowing is simple. You pilot the machine back and forth, while your mind is a thousand miles away. But down at ground level, those whirling blades are administering a shock to countless thousands of plants. All too often homeowners are unaware of the one-third rule, which states that you should not cut off more than one-third of the blades' length with a single mowing session.

How much is one-third? You can judge it by eye, but I prefer occasionally getting down on my hands and knees with a ruler. Measure the height of the grass before mowing, make a test cut, then measure again. If the lawn had been 3 in. high, it should now

be 2 in. Measuring is also valuable because it helps you learn *when* to cut.

Why is this so important? Doesn't mowing serve the same purpose as a haircut? Not really. The leaves are the part of the grass plant that generates sugars and carbohydrates. If most of the leaf tissue is suddenly

THE ONE-THIRD RULE

It's a simple rule but important to remember: If you scalp the grass, the lawn will suffer.

Don't remove more than one-third of the grass's length.

3 in.   2 in.

TURF TIP

Don't Get in a Rut

Mow in a different direction each time you cut the grass to avoid having the wheels create ruts in the lawn.

TOOL TALK | **KEEP SHARP!**

IF YOU MOW A GOOD-SIZE LAWN, the blade may need sharpening once a month. You'll know when you've put it off too long—a close inspection will show that the cut grass blades have fuzzy ends. These ends not only look unattractive but are entry points for disease.

You may be able to transport a small rotary mower to the shop for regular servicing, sharpening included. But if you have a tractor mower, the service people may have to call on you. Or, if you are handy with a wrench, you can remove the blade, then either take it in for sharpening or do the job at home.

Before removing the blade, be sure to pull the spark-plug wire off the plug to make sure that the engine won't start. Use a wrench to loosen the nut securing the blade. Place the blade in a bench vise and go over its beveled edge with a flat file. Be careful to maintain the angle of this edge. If it's too blunt, grass will be torn and frayed, even when the blade is sharp; if

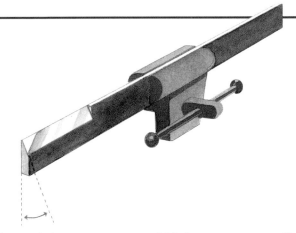

the angle is too acute, around 20 degrees or so, you'll get a reasonable cut but the blade will dull quickly.

A blade is apt to take a beating on all but the most manicured of lawns, so inspect it before sharpening. If the blade appears bent or is heavily dinged by stones, then it makes sense to buy a replacement; as parts go, blades are inexpensive.

Trimming

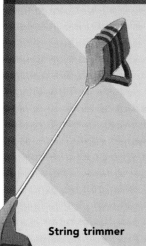

String trimmer

In a perfect landscape, there would be no need for string trimmers. But I have yet to see one that wouldn't benefit from being trimmed at least occasionally. Trimming is time-consuming—and this is a good reason to avoid creating thin, narrow strips of lawn and sharp corners when laying out a lawn.

Before you trim, dress the part. You'll need to wear long pants, protective eyewear, and substantial shoes at the minimum. Trimmers can pick up and hurl small rocks and debris at your body at great speed.

Use caution around trees and shrubs, making sure you don't let the nylon string come in contact with the trunk. The living layer of the bark can be destroyed in seconds, depriving the tree of the nutrients and water it needs to survive. By ringing each tree with mulch, you can avoid close trimming. Don't place the mulch right up next to the trunk, however, or you may encourage basal root rot; leave a gap of 2 in. or 3 in.

COMMON MISTAKE

Sharpening a Reel Mower

It isn't all that challenging to sharpen the blade of a rotary mower, but if you have a reel mower, leave the job to the dealer or a sharpening service.

Homeowners commonly remove too much grass with each mowing. Until you learn to eyeball blade length, it's a good idea to measure how much you're removing.

lopped off, the plant has to rely on stored energy reserves to produce more leaves. When this happens week after week, the plants weaken, becoming more susceptible to pests and drought stress.

To follow the one-third rule, you may have to either raise the blade or increase your mowing frequency, depending on how fast the lawn is growing. In the North, spring and fall weather encourage rapid growth. The same is true for spring and summer in the South. This could mean you'll find yourself mowing twice a week—and if you have a large lawn, that may be more work than you care to invest. There's no easy answer, other than moving to a condo. Consider either replacing the existing grass with a low-maintenance species (see chapter 7) or planting part of the lawn to ground covers that take care of themselves.

If you miss a week of mowing, don't compound the problem by forgetting to raise the mower. Keep the one-third rule in mind, raising the deck so that you will be taking off no more than the top third of the blades.

Mowing through the seasons

The old approach to lawn care had it that you'd mow *low* in spring and fall and *high* in the heat of summer. There's some logic to that. As the mowing height is raised, the roots respond by growing deeper and do a better job of supplying the grass plants with water in the summer heat.

Current research suggests that there are other factors at work. By raising the height of the cut, you leave more of the leaf, and that may mean more water is lost to the atmosphere. It also may be that the higher the grass, the thinner the grass. The compromise is to raise the mower only a moderate amount—to create some shade for the plants—and to mow more often as necessary.

Usually, I don't like to compromise; however, in this case, it makes sense. So, in the heat of summer, raise the height 20 percent to 30 percent. The one thing that doesn't change is the frequency, which is governed by the one-third rule. When the grass grows 33 percent taller, it's time to mow.

How to deal with clippings

The one-third rule has another advantage. If you don't take a great deal off with each mowing, you won't produce a lot of clippings at any one time. That's good news, because a heavy accumulation of clippings has to be disposed of, for a couple of reasons: The lawn will look like a miniature hay field, and the yard just can't absorb all that green matter.

The best (and easiest) thing to do with clippings is allow them to stay right where they fall, and you can do that with a mulching mower. These models reduce clippings to a size that the soil can break down easily. This spares you the hassle of either raking or dumping the contents of a clip-

---

TURF TIP

Mowing Strips Save Time

Border trees, flower beds, and walls with a mowing strip of brick, stone pavers, or mulch to establish a crisp edge around the lawn and reduce the need for string trimming.

TOOL TALK **SEASON-END MOWER MAINTENANCE**

WHEN COLD WEATHER APPROACHES, most of us are happy to forget all about yard work. But before you hibernate for the winter, take care of the mower's maintenance needs.

- Drain the gasoline. If left in the gas tank over the winter, it becomes gummy. (Another option is to start the mower and let it run until the tank goes dry.)

- Drain the oil from the mower, and replace it with fresh oil. Clean or replace the oil filter. Check the air filter, if necessary.

- Deal responsibly with old oil and leftover gas by bringing them to a service shop for disposal.

- Disconnect the spark plug, remove the blade, and use a putty knife and screwdriver to loosen caked-on grass from under the mower deck.

- Sharpen the blade (see "Keep Sharp!" on p. 55), then check it for balance by setting it on a golf ball or other round object. If the blade doesn't rest horizontally, file away metal from the heavier side until it is balanced.

- Use a deep-socket wrench to remove the spark plug. If the tip is blackened or the electrode is worn, replace the plug as recommended in the owner's manual. Set the gap with a feeler gauge, as specified in the manual or on the spark-plug package.

TURF TIP

Get a Jump on the Season

In spring, the lawn tends to resume growing well before it shows signs of life. Give the yard an early mowing to remove winter's browned blades and reveal the mostly green grass below.

TURF TIP

Mulching Mowers

Don't be turned off to mulching mowers if you've had a bad experience with an early model. They were undersize and tended to clog up. Today's mowers have enough power to cut clippings finely and efficiently, so you won't see that telltale row of clippings.

pings bag. (Actually, as long as the one-third rule is followed, this works with the standard side-discharge types, as well. The mulching models just cut the clippings into finer pieces and don't blow them as far.) Grass clippings have a modest amount of fertilizer value, providing from one-fourth to one-third of the lawn's nitrogen requirement, for no added work or expense.

Of course, if you do gather clippings, you should not put them out with the trash. Take advantage of your local recycling program, or recycle them right on your property. Many vegetable gardeners like to use grass clippings for mulch between rows. Others add them to the compost pile. (If your lawn is infected with a foliar disease, it's a good idea to remove the clippings to avoid further inoculating the grass with spores from the leaf blades. Composting is the best option here, as the decomposition process will kill most foliar pathogens.) If the lawn has been

treated recently with herbicides, don't use the clippings to mulch around plants at the risk of damaging them.

A Fertilizing Primer

Grass plants need to draw more than a dozen elements from the soil. Most yards are deficient in at least one, and that means fertilizing in order to grow a good-looking lawn. In order to know just what you should be placing on the lawn, you'll need to learn its particular strengths and weaknesses. (Refer back to chapter 2 for a discussion on how to order a test for your soil.) Most lawns will turn out to be low in nitrogen. The good news is that in many areas of the country, nitrogen is the only nutrient that you'll have to supplement. If your soil has other shortcomings, check fertilizer labels to find a product that meets your needs.

One of the first things you notice about a fertilizer bag is the series of three numbers on the front side. These numbers indicate how much nitrogen, phosphorous, and potassium (in that order) is in the bag. For example, a product with the nutrient analysis of 28-2-4 contains 28 percent nitrogen, 2 percent phosphorous, and 4 percent potassium.

There's more to a fertilizer than the numbers on the bag, however. If you buy a really inexpensive bag of lawn food, you'll be getting a quick-release product that makes its nitrogen available in a hurry. As a result, the

Down at this level, the lawn feels the impact of a mowing more than you may realize. By removing no more than one-third of the blades at a time, you will minimize stress to the plants.

Well-timed fertilizer applications encourage a healthy lawn. Properly nourished turfs crowd out weeds, ward off pests, and are striking to look at.

lawn usually will turn bright green within a few days after an application and produce lots of top growth. That may sound good, but the results last only two or three weeks on average, and you'll have to mow more often to keep up with the flush of growth. Foliar diseases are more likely to develop, and there is the increased chance that excess fertilizer will run off and pollute water supplies.

In a quick-release bag, the nitrogen will be supplied by urea, ammonium nitrate, or ammonium sulfate. Instead, look for a slow-release fertilizer that contains sulfur-coated urea, methylene urea, urea formaldehyde, isobutylidene diurea (IBDU®), or water-insoluble nitrogen. These provide nutrients to the lawn gradually over a six- to eight-week period. The fertilizer produces a mod-

NITROGEN SOURCES	
Slow-Release Products	**Fast-Release Products**
Isobutylidene diurea [IBDU]	Urea
Urea formaldehyde	Ammonium sulfate
Methylene urea	Ammonium nitrate
Milorganite	Sodium nitrate
Water-insoluble nitrogen	
Sulfur-coated urea	
Feather meal	
Bonemeal	
Processed tankage	

TURF TIP

Off-Season Spreading

Use your lawn spreader in the winter to scatter sawdust, sand, or deicers on a slippery sidewalk and driveway. Keep in mind that deicers may be caustic on moving parts and damaging to adjacent lawn areas.

est increase in growth rate and a negligible pollution potential. Ideally, shop for a product offering a mixture of about one-fourth to one-third quick-release fertilizer and the rest slow release. This will provide immediate help for an anemic lawn, with long-lasting benefits as well.

Organic nitrogen sources are also good options. Feather meal, bonemeal, dried sewage sludge, blood meal, and alfalfa meal are examples of ingredients that offer a quality, slow-release feeding. A downside to these nitrogen sources is that they require an active microorganism population in the soil to break them down into a usable form. This occurs only at soil temperatures above 50°F, so organic nitrogen products are not good choices in midspring or late fall (see the chart on p. 64 for suggested feeding times).

Fertilizing gear

There are three ways to spread fertilizer around the yard, all with their own advantages and cautions. The implements used for each are inexpensive, so choosing a method won't be an intimidating decision.

A drop spreader simply allows the fertilizer to fall out of a hopper as you wheel the thing along. The fertilizer is applied in a narrow strip between the tires. You must be careful to be guided by the tracks you've left in the lawn; otherwise, gaps in coverage will show up as stripes of paler green. A drop spreader gives you a lot of control, but the work goes fairly slowly, and that can be a real drawback if you have a large yard.

A rotary spreader distributes the fertilizer by centrifugal force. It does the job in about one-fifth of the time that it would take with a drop spreader. Because of the broad pattern over which the fertilizer is scattered,

there is less chance of leaving untreated strips of lawn. For most lawns, a wheeled rotary spreader is best, but small handheld models will work for limited areas.

Fertilizer can also be distributed through a jet of water by using a hose-end sprayer, a technique introduced by lawn-care companies. The product is placed in a reservoir attached to a garden hose. There are no great advantages to applying fertilizer this way. Lawn-care companies use sprayers for their flexibility and speed over a long day of applying lawn chemicals; herbicides, wetting agents, and fertilizers can be applied at the same time. With only one lawn to treat, however, these advantages just don't matter that much.

What's more, a number of things can go wrong when using a hose-end sprayer. The units marketed to the homeowner tend to be imprecise, so that it often is difficult to apply the product where you want it. Because the spray typically is applied to the side while walking along, it's also something of a challenge to direct the coverage. Finally, you've got that hose to drag around.

FERTILIZING EQUIPMENT

Drop spreader

TURF TIP

A Spreader for an Edgy Lawn

Does your yard have a lot of nooks, crannies, sidewalks, and such? You'll get precise spreading of seed and fertilizer with a drop spreader.

A drop spreader doesn't deliver much seed, fertilizer, or compost with each pass, but it distributes the goods with accuracy.

Handheld rotary spreader

Wheeled rotary spreader

Because a rotary spreader broadcasts over a considerable area, it is suited to seeding or fertilizing a large lawn.

A Driveway Test Run

To see just how evenly your spreader is spreading, put a small amount of fertilizer in the hopper and make a short pass on the driveway. If the pattern is distorted, check the spreader for rust, caked fertilizer particles, and yard debris.

Put it on smart

"Put it on smart" is a phrase I use when describing how to apply lawn-care products in a way that won't cause pollution or waste your time and money. You'll have to use a bit of math—although it's just elementary-level number crunching. Begin by measuring your lawn, following the estimating procedure

WHAT YOU'LL NEED

Applying Fertilizer

✓ Calculator
✓ Tape measure
✓ Small countertop or postal scale
✓ Fertilizer spreader
✓ Bag of fertilizer

described in chapter 1. Next, consult the chart on the facing page to determine how much fertilizer you should be spreading.

It is likely that your spreader, even if it's brand new, isn't set up accurately. To ensure you will be applying the right level of fertilizer, do some fine tuning. Weigh out the amount of fertilizer needed to cover 1,000 sq. ft., and put it in the spreader. Set the spreader to the number recommended by the manufacturer. Then spread away (preferably on a part of the lawn that is not particularly visible, in case the calibration is considerably off). Depending on whether you run out of fertilizer or have some left over, adjust the spreader as necessary. You could do the test on a smaller area, but it's much harder to be accurate with smaller areas and product volumes.

HOSE-END APPLICATOR

When spreading fertilizer or seed, be sure to walk at the same rate over the whole lawn. If you start to rush things, you'll put down a light distribution, and the results of your haste may be visible a few weeks down the road.

After fertilizing the lawn, water it lightly to wash the product off leaf surfaces and down to the soil. If you skip this step, you might notice burnt-looking grass plants, caused by fertilizer particles drawing water out of the leaves.

When to fertilize

Knowing when to fertilize is just as important as how to apply it. See the chart on p. 64 for holidays that can serve as reminders of application dates.

Each application has its own purpose or objective for the lawn. For cool-season lawns, a light dose (0.5 lb.) of nitrogen, given on Tax Day, will encourage moderate but controlled growth. Around Memorial Day, the lawn is entering a stressful period (summer), so a moderate (1.0-lb.) application of nitrogen with an equal dose of potassium will provide what's needed to help the lawn

grow well. In early fall, the lawn is thickening so it needs a moderate slow-release nitrogen feeding. A heavy (1.5-lb. to 2.0-lb.) dose of slow-release nitrogen with potassium is suitable for the Halloween time frame. For warm-season grasses, the goal is to provide

Don't guess how much fertilizer to put in the spreader. It's easy to calculate the amount.

NITROGEN NUMBERS

Here is a quick guide to determine how many pounds of fertilizer with a nutrient analysis of 24-2-5 that you'd need to deliver various amounts of nitrogen to 1,000 sq. ft. of lawn.

Nitrogen [lb.]	Fertilizer [lb.]
1.5	6.25
1.25	5.2
1.0	4.2
0.75	3.1
0.50	2.1

three equal, moderate (1-lb.) doses in spring and summer.

You can go by the chart and do a good job of fertilizing, but there are times when you may want to adapt your procedure:

- Apply fertilizer to help the lawn snap back from disease, drought, or insects, once the problem has been treated.

- Take advantage of the fact that fertilizing will be most effective after a session of aeration and power-raking.

- Avoid fertilization during a drought, especially on a low-maintenance lawn.

- In the North, allow the lawn to go dormant by ending applications a month before mowing is finished for the year. Then, after the final mowing, fertilize one last time to encourage the lawn to build up its root system.

- Use lighter-than-normal applications to lawns with a history of leaf spot (melting out), brown patch, and pythium blight, and use heavier-than-normal applications to lawns with a history of dollar spot.

When feeding your lawn, early morning is better than midday. Your spreader will leave tracks in the morning dew, making it easier to see where you've been. And wind speeds are lower at that time of day, so there's less chance of the fertilizer blowing around.

Watering Wisdom

Water is such a simple substance, and yet the lawn is dependent on the right amount of it, applied at the right time. Overwatering not only encourages root rot and compaction but is also a waste of a precious resource. Underwatering produces a thin lawn, decreased rooting depth, and stunted grass plants.

How do you know when a lawn is thirsty? Walk across the yard, then return a few minutes later: If you see your footprints, then the grass blades are lacking sufficient moisture to stand up straight, and chances are watering is in order. Another test is to probe the soil. Push a screwdriver or trowel into the lawn. If it doesn't go in easily, your grass is probably dry and in need of water.

FEEDING TIME FOR THE LAWN

When should you spread fertilizer? Here are dates that should help you remember this key event in your lawn's year.

TYPE OF GRASS: Cool-season grasses like Kentucky bluegrass, perennial ryegrass, tall fescue, fine fescue	TYPE OF GRASS: Warm-season grasses like zoysiagrass, bermudagrass, St. Augustinegrass, centipedegrass
GENERAL TIMES OF YEAR	**GENERAL TIMES OF YEAR**
▪ Tax Day	▪ Two weeks after green-up (when new growth has resumed)
▪ Memorial Day	▪ Memorial Day
▪ Labor Day	▪ 4th of July
▪ Halloween	

Water is to grass as food is to a person. Too little or too much causes problems. Your job is to apply just the right amount.

Try to avoid evening and nighttime watering sessions. The grass blades remain wet and cool, setting up conditions that favor foliar diseases. The morning hours, from four to noon, are the best time to water. The grass blades are able to dry as the day warms up, discouraging diseases. Afternoon application is adequate, but the water tends to evaporate more readily and blow to where it isn't needed.

The key is to water to the bottom of the root system, no matter how deep it is. A regular watering schedule normally would call for an application every three days to five days in spring and fall and every two days to three days in summer. If your lawn is on a slope, lighter and more frequent sprinklings will prevent runoff and waste of water.

Hose attachments

There are all sorts of fixtures, simple and high tech, that can be attached to a faucet or the end of a hose to distribute water. As you might expect, the simpler devices are inexpensive but somewhat inaccurate, while the high-tech ones are more costly but much more water efficient. My advice: Invest in a quality sprinkler, either in ground or with a hose attached; you won't regret it.

A soaker hose is simply a hose with tiny holes that slowly deliver water to a narrow area. Oscillating sprinklers cover a rectangular area that can be adjusted more or less,

TURF TIP

When to Water
When the lawn loses its normal green color and takes on a bluish purple tinge, it may be time to get out the sprinkler.

You can water the lawn by pressing your thumb against the end of the hose, but an ever-increasing number of devices will do a better job of spraying water where you want it, when you want it.

TURF TIP

Water to the Roots

To get the hang of how long to water, probe the soil after a session with the hose or sprinkler. Ideally, the soil will be moist to ½ in. below the deepest roots.

If the lawn is flat, then take advantage of the rain train's feature: low drift potential, low evaporation, and slow but steady water delivery.

depending on the model's features. Impact sprinklers rotate to deliver water in a circle or part of a circle. Both sprinklers tend to allow a substantial amount of water to drift off the lawn on a windy day.

Intrigued by clever gadgets? You can buy a little self-propelled watering tractor that creeps across the lawn, delivering droplets of water close to the ground. These "rain trains" are effective only on relatively flat and rectangular or square lawns.

In-ground systems

Automatic in-ground systems are convenient. There are no hoses to bother with, and a controller can be set to allow the system to run at certain times each day. Some systems use geared rotors, which rotate back and forth horizontally. Stream rotors operate in a circular fashion. Fixed spray heads pop out of the ground and deliver a fine spray of water in a circle, a portion of a circle, or a narrow strip—without having to be moved. You can order a sprinkler system that incorporates several types of heads to handle various features of your yard. The best time to install a system is when putting in a new lawn (but after construction is completed, to avoid damaging the heads). Obviously, you can install one in an existing lawn, but being able to use an automatic system to help establish a new lawn sure beats dragging hoses through mud!

Can a system water the lawn as well as a person using hoses and sprinklers? Absolutely. Systems deliver water in a mist, rather than a heavy spray, so that the lawn can absorb more with little waste. The timer function of the controller allows you to go on vacation without worry. This isn't to say that an in-ground water system works for everyone. The cost is considerable. And if your region gets a lot of rain or if the yard is small, you may want to make do with end-of-the-hose portable sprinklers.

Testing a watering system

No matter what means you use to water your lawn—a hose attachment or an in-ground system—it's a good idea to run a simple test of just how evenly it is doing its job.

Place several empty cans around the area that will be sprayed, and run the water for 10 minutes or so. Then go around noting how much has been collected in each can. Don't be disappointed if there are different amounts—no sprinkling system can give each square foot an equal dose. But take big differences into consideration. With hose-end portables, you may have to plan on overlapping coverage as you move the unit around the lawn. With an in-ground system, you can adjust the heads or use different types of heads to improve distribution.

To ensure that you get good coverage with a hose-end sprinkler, move it in a consistent pattern. For a reasonably rectangular lawn, rotate the sprinkler to the four corners, as illustrated, and you'll be less likely to leave an area short on water.

In-ground watering systems can be fitted with several types of heads to distribute water in patterns to suit your particular yard. A gear-driven system offers larger droplets and a consistent distribution pattern, resulting in more water on the lawn and less in the street, especially if it's a little windy.

TOOL TALK   HOSE SCIENCE

FOR LAWN WATERING, purchase a ⅝-in. or ¾-in. hose. A ½-in. lightweight hose won't deliver water quickly enough. The hose should be made of several layers of material—a thin inner core, netting, and a thick outer core. If you live in the North, bring hoses in for the winter to avoid damage from freezing. Or, if you don't have the storage space, drain the hoses and stow them under cover.

If it's well adjusted, an in-ground system is a water saver as well as a convenience.

ROTATE YOUR SPRINKLER

To avoid missing patches of lawn, take the time to move hose-attachment sprinklers each time you water the lawn.

Watering in a short-term drought

A lawn can survive drought by storing water in the crowns, rhizomes, and stolons. These may be the only parts of the plant that remain alive as the blades turn yellow. Then, when water is made available again, the plants are able to send up new shoots, re-establishing the lawn. Here are some strategies for managing a lawn during periods of drought.

- **Encourage dormancy.** If you completely withhold water and there is no natural source, then plants will die. However, by applying one-fourth to one-third of the water that you'd normally use, the lawn will stay alive by going dormant. Dormant grass plants aren't very attractive, but at least you can look forward to a green lawn once the rains return.

- **Fertilize less.** Fertilizer encourages growth, which creates a lot of leaf surface area from which to lose water. Use greatly reduced rates of slow-release nitrogen fertilizer to keep the turf alive without producing a great number of new shoots.

- **Mow less often.** Freshly cut blades lose water through their open ends.

- **Sharpen the mower blade.** Dull blades tend to rip and tear grass blades, creating larger openings through which water can evaporate.

- **Raise the mower.** Raise the blade 20 percent or so to create a "canopy effect" that will help shade the lawn from the drying effects of the sun and wind.

- **Don't remove clippings from the lawn.** A light sprinkling of grass clippings will act as a mulch for the grass plants, holding in soil moisture and keeping the crowns cooler.

- **Designate a "hydrozone."** Create a maintenance hierarchy between high- and low-maintenance lawn areas. Use your precious water resources on the small areas where the kids play games and where you entertain guests. Allow the rest of the lawn to go dormant.

- **Don't edge the lawn.** Edging creates more openings in grass blades than mowing, and this means greater moisture loss.

- **Keep off the grass.** Restrict traffic to the high-maintenance hydrozone. Traffic bruises grass blades and increases moisture loss.

- **Lay off the herbicide.** Herbicides stress the grass plants a bit. Instead, simply pull the weeds or let them be. You can worry about weed control when the drought is over.

When Is Rain Enough?

The ideal way to water your lawn is to let nature do it. Rain is free and applied uniformly (except for under trees, that is). You can use a rain gauge to measure what falls from above, and adjust your own watering schedule accordingly. In summer, figure that your lawn will need from 1 in. to 2 in. of water per week. In spring and fall, half that amount will do.

Watering in a long-term drought

Your strategies may change if you expect to be going through a long dry spell, including planting an entirely new type of grass.

- **Switch grasses.** Replace the lawn with a cultivar known for getting by on less water. Consider centipedegrass, buffalograss, or zoysiagrass to take the place of bermudagrass, perennial ryegrass, or Kentucky bluegrass.

- **Improve the soil.** Facilitate drainage and encourage root growth by adding compost and improving aeration. For best results, go to the trouble of stripping off the existing turf, make the changes, and then reseed or resod.

- **Control thatch.** Use routine aeration and power-raking to reduce the level of thatch; this makes it easier for water to reach the roots.

- **Winterize.** You can prepare for next year's drought season by applying a heavy rate of fertilizer as the grass is going dormant in late fall. This encourages deeper roots, which in turn will improve the ability of the lawn to make use of the small amount of water it receives.

TURF TIP

A Slant on Watering

Water applied to a steeply sloped lawn tends to run to the bottom without soaking in. Operate the sprinkler until you notice water trickling away, wait three hours, then water again; water a third time if necessary. A sprinkler timer will make this routine a lot easier.

CHAPTER 5

Dealing with Thatch

Aerating

Overseeding

OTHER LAWN CHORES

L AWNS MEAN MOWING. They also mean watering and an occasional dose of fertilizer. That's where it stops for many of us. But there are other jobs you can do that, without much effort on your part, will yield a better-than-average lawn. These tasks address problems that are apt to develop so gradually that it's easy to overlook them: a buildup of thatch, an overall thinness, and a general decline.

Dealing with Thatch

Thatch is one of those lawn troubles you never really see. It's an interwoven layer of mostly dead roots, crowns, and stems, located between the soil and the green lawn. Although thatch is usually spoken of as a problem, along with weeds and bugs, you wouldn't want to be entirely without it (see the sidebar on the facing page). The trouble starts when thatch is allowed to build up.

As the layer approaches 1 in. in thickness, roots tend to grow into the thatch rather than reach into the soil. And although thatch can be a good environment for quick, easy

A bit of thatch is good, but a lot can mean trouble. To monitor how thick the layer is, measure annually in a few spots around the lawn.

growth if moist, when it dries out (as it will with summer temperatures), the grass wilts and is apt to die as the heat bakes the roots. Even plenty of water won't remedy the condition.

Disease and insect problems are aggravated by excess thatch. Sod webworms and black cutworms like to live there; fungal diseases such as bipolaris leaf spot, summer patch, and dollar spot also thrive here. Then, if you apply a pesticide or fungicide, the thatch makes things difficult by absorbing much of the active ingredients so that they can't do their job.

Slowing thatch buildup

One way to avoid thatch problems is to slow its buildup. You can do a lot to reduce thatch

Small areas can be easily prepared with a thatching rake.

THATCH LAYER

Many grass species produce thatch naturally, and this layer can become a problem as the root system grows into the thatch rather than into the soil.

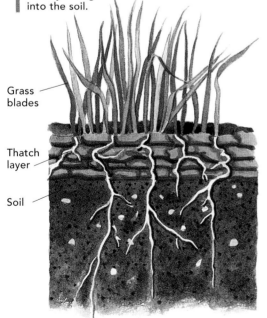

Grass blades

Thatch layer

Soil

How Much Thatch Is Too Much?

The thatch layer is apt to become a problem if it accumulates at a rate faster than ⅛ in. per year; the ideal thickness is about ½ in. Here are a few indications that you've got more than enough:

- when you notice a greater-than-average incidence of disease and insect problems;
- when grass dries out and dies during hot, dry weather;
- when the lawn feels spongy underfoot, as if you're walking on pillows.

The only way to tell for sure is to cut a core sample. Use a sharp spade to remove a core, at least 3 in. deep, and measure the thatch layer. When the layer reaches ¾ in., consider dethatching.

Water Less Often?

Are you one of those maintenance lovers who waters the lawn every day, without fail? You may be encouraging the buildup of thatch. Watering daily can contribute to this problem if it means that the moisture never penetrates beyond a shallow depth.

A power rake can make short work of dethatching a lawn, and it's well worth the expense of a day's rental.

Thatch Isn't All Bad

Thatch does have some benefits—you don't want to banish it from your yard. That layer can act like the pad under your carpet. By cushioning the lawn, it prevents the grass crowns (where the growing point is located) from being crushed by foot traffic. Thatch also helps to conserve the soil's moisture. As it decomposes, organic matter is introduced to the soil below, making life more pleasant for earthworms and other beneficial soil organisms. If you happen to mistakenly apply too much pesticide, the thatch layer will absorb much of the excess rather than allowing it to run into the street or storm sewer.

buildup by changing cultural and environmental practices:

- Select a grass species that forms less thatch, such as perennial ryegrass or tall fescue.

- Avoid overfertilization.

- Keep the soil pH between 6.0 and 7.0.

- When mowing, remove no more than one-third of the plant at a time.

- Bag clippings or use a mulching mower.

- To encourage soil bacteria and fungi to break down thatch naturally, use insecticides sparingly.

Removing thatch

Thatch just won't go away by itself; its components break down extremely slowly. A thatching rake and a little elbow grease might be enough to manage a thin layer of thatch on a small lawn. This is a tool with a few dozen blades that comb out some of the thatch. For a large lawn, especially one with a thatch layer thicker than 1 in., rent a power dethacher or, for dense-growing bermudagrass or zoysia, a vertical mower. Make sure the soil is moist but not wet. Even with a gas motor doing a lot of the work, dethatching isn't easy—your muscles will feel it the next day.

To avoid injuring the lawn, do not remove more than ½ in. of the thatch layer at one time; because live plants are yanked out along with the thatch, it may take the lawn a while to recover from a dethatching session. Also, do the work during a time of year when the lawn will be quick to snap back. For cool-season lawns, early fall is best. Early spring is also acceptable, especially if the thatch is so thick that you'll be dethatching a second time that fall. Repeat this seasonal process until the thatch layer is down to ½ in.

Warm-season lawns of zoysia, bermuda, centipede, or St. Augustine should be dethatched in late spring to early summer because plants are actively growing at that time.

COMMON MISTAKE

Dethatching Attachments

Stay away from dethatching attachments that are sold as add-on contraptions for lawn mowers. These devices tend to be cheaply made and don't hold up well to repeated use.

These blades spin vertically to pull excess thatch and other debris from the lawn.

Aerating

It's hard to imagine that punching holes in anything would make it better, but most lawns benefit from occasional aeration. The point is to improve the roots' neighborhood by loosening the soil around them and giving them more access to oxygen and nutrients. Aeration also slows the buildup of thatch because it helps microorganisms work more efficiently at breaking down this plant material. It's best to aerate cool-season lawns in the fall and spring—in September, April, October, and May—and warm-season lawns in the early summer (June).

You can aerate a small lawn by hand with a corer, a tool with two or three hollow tines that you push into the ground and then lift to remove cores of lawn. It works, but it's slow. More reasonable is to rent a power aerator. As you go over the lawn with this tool, cores of soil, thatch, and grass plants are plucked out and tossed behind the unit.

Microorganisms will help break down thatch in the cores. To encourage these beneficial fungi and bacteria, allow the cores to dry for a couple of days on top of the lawn, then mow slowly to thoroughly chop up and distribute them. Over the next few weeks, both soil and microorganisms will be carried down into the thatch layer by rain and watering. Think of this layer as something like a flat compost pile in which decomposition is going on.

A word of caution: Aeration is messy. Those cores litter the lawn until they dry out and can be reincorporated, so you won't want this procedure to coincide with a lawn party.

BENEFITS OF AERATION

By removing cores in soil that is compacted, you allow roots to grow more deeply.

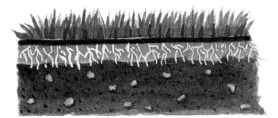

Compacted top 2 in.

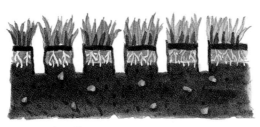

Aeration process removes cores.

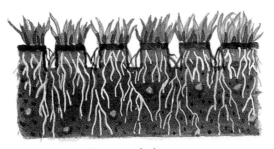

Roots reach deeper.

CORER

A power aerator (above) pulls hundreds of plugs from your lawn, creating openings for water and air.

These plugs of soil and sod (left) will soon break apart and be assimilated into the lawn, where they will help to slow down the buildup of thatch.

By overseeding, you can turn a thin lawn into something your neighbors admire.

Overseeding

There comes a time in the life of most lawns when they start to look a little thin. Perhaps dry conditions or a bit of foliar disease have caused some grass plants to die, leaving the lawn looking a bit ragged. If so, consider overseeding—scattering seed over an existing lawn.

The best time for overseeding is in late summer or early fall for cool-season grasses and late spring for warm-season grasses. Because the existing lawn will compete with the new grass for water, sunlight, and nutrients, you can increase the new blades' chances by mowing the lawn very low before overseeding. Really scalp it—generally, at half the recommended height. This serves both to admit more light and also to stress the existing grass plants slightly. Consider hiring a lawn service to apply a plant growth regulator (such as Primo® or Embark®) to further suppress the existing lawn.

Follow the close mowing with cultivation, readying the soil for the new seed. The worse the lawn's condition, the more extensively you need to cultivate to create a good seedbed. Aeration and power-raking will help ensure good seed-to-soil contact. To expose enough soil for the seed, be sure to aerate in several directions—the first two passes at right angles to each other and the third on a diagonal. When power-raking, several passes may also be necessary. It's important to leave some stubble or sturdy grass plants behind to prevent erosion, keep seed in place, and shade new seedlings.

Alternatively, you can hire a lawn service to carry out either one of two procedures:

- **Slicing.** If you've ever seen a farmer discing a field prior to planting corn or soybeans, then you've seen a big-scale version of slicing. The lawn service will use a machine with rows of circular blades to cut thin grooves into the lawn, creating openings for the seed to fall into. (You may be able to carry out this job yourself by renting a power slicer.)

- **Slit seeding.** With this method, the power tool both slices into the soil and sows the seed. Slit seeding may be costly, but it normally produces good results, especially if several passes are made over the lawn.

Choose disease-resistant seed whenever possible. One of the best methods of controlling summer patch, leaf spot, dollar spot, and other diseases is to use a grass that is genetically resistant to the pathogen. Check with your local extension agent for the latest data on how well certain cultivars grow in your area.

Seed the lawn as discussed in chapter 3. Water frequently and lightly for the first two weeks or so after seeding. Gradually reduce the frequency and increase the length of watering periods to help form a durable root system.

Delay applications of starter fertilizer until three weeks after the overseeding to encourage the rapid establishment of the new seedlings. If applied at seeding time, the fertilizer increases the growth of the existing grass plants, and they might become vigorous enough to shade out the seedlings.

TOOL TALK GIVE YOUR LAWN AN EDGE

A POWER EDGER can be used to give your yard a clean, sharp line, especially where driveways, sidewalks, and patios join the lawn. If you are after a moderate- to high-maintenance yard, consider either buying or renting one of these specialty tools.

The process of edging slices many plants in half, leaving the remaining part vulnerable to drying. To avoid creating nice, straight, brown edges, carry out this job at a cool, moist time of the year.

PROBLEM SOLVING

T SOME POINT, ALL LAWNS HAVE TROUBLE WITH PESTS or adverse environmental conditions. It's inevitable. To find the reason, you'll need to do a bit of detective work. The skills aren't all that different from determining why your car won't start or what is responsible for your child's stomachache. And fortunately, most of the problems have relatively easy solutions.

Diagnosis Comes First

Let's say your lawn has a brown or thin area. What's causing it? At first, you might feel overwhelmed—there are so many possible causes—and a lawn, unlike a child, can't tell you where it hurts. Start by looking at the problem up close. Get down on your hands and knees and poke around. You can't learn much by surveying the lawn from your patio.

Is the affected area small and localized? That suggests it could be the result of local conditions, such as heavy shade, too much heat, or salt from an adjacent driveway. Or

If you want to see what might be going on under the sod, take a peek. Underground feeders make it easy to lift a patch of lawn because they eat the grass roots.

are you looking at a large, widespread area? Sweeping changes tend to be the work of insects or diseases. Keep this difference in mind when considering possible causes.

Is It a Bug Problem?

The easiest problems to identify tend to be those caused by insects. In some cases dousing the soil with lemon-scented detergent, as explained in the next section, will flush out bugs so that you can identify them. There are three basic groups of insect pests:

- Surface feeders that suck plant juices, such as clover mites, leafhoppers, and chinch bugs.

- Surface feeders that eat leaves and crowns, such as sod webworms, armyworms, cutworms, and fiery skippers.

- Underground feeders, such as grubs, wireworms, and mole crickets.

Surface feeders

Lawn pests differ not only in how they eat but also in where they do their dirty work—aboveground or out of sight beneath the soil.

The easiest bugs to identify are those that feed on the surface. Here is a handy way to spot them. Mix ¼ cup of lemon-scented dishwashing soap in 2 gal. of water, and use a watering can to sprinkle this solution over a square of lawn that's about 3 ft. on a side. This treatment will irritate the surface feeders, causing them to leave their hiding places in the thatch so that you can see them. Wait about 5 min. to 10 min. and then count the insects. If you see more than one type of insect, make separate counts of each.

Large numbers of insects can cause damage. At the first sign of lawn injury, consider treatment. With a few years of experience, you'll find that 10 to 20 webworms and 20 to 30 armyworms per square yard merit serious attention.

These pests are readily killed with foliar insecticides, applied with a hose-end sprayer or pressure tank. These preparations work best when the spray contacts bugs while they're feeding.

Underground feeders

If you spot only a few surface feeders, or none at all, then move on to look for underground feeders that attack the roots of grass plants. They tend to be larvae—grubs or worms—rather than adult bugs with wings and legs. To inspect an affected patch of lawn, roll back a bit of the grass. Use a

TURF TIP

Bird Alert
If you see lots of starlings, crows, or grackles pecking away at your lawn, it might be a sign of an insect invasion. Inspect the lawn for sod webworms, armyworms, cutworms, or white grubs, and take control measures if they are at a damaging level.

Getting Help

All of this scratching in the lawn for bugs may leave you scratching your head as well if you can't identify a problem. Don't fret, help is a phone call or short drive away. Call on a county cooperative extension horticulturist or a Master Gardener working through the cooperative extension. You can find them in the phone book under the government listings for "Agricultural Extension" or "County Extension."

pocketknife to cut down into the sod in a straight line for 4 in. to 6 in., then cut at a right angle to make an L. Peel back the resulting flap, and have a look.

As with surface feeders, treat at the first sign of lawn injury: 5 to 10 masked chafer grubs and 25 to 50 black turfgrass aetenius grubs per square yard

Pesticides

Pesticides are any agents used to kill pests—whether they are considered "organic" or "synthetic." Generally, organic pesticides are less toxic than synthetic ones—but not always. They may be a good first choice for controlling a lawn pest and may work well in many situations. However, there are some categories of pests where organic pesticides simply won't work. Certain species of white grubs, many weeds, and most diseases don't have an effective organic option.

The key when using any pesticide is to read and follow explicitly the directions on the label. The label will list mixing instructions, applicator clothing requirements, timing for application, restrictions (if any) for humans or pets to re-enter the lawn after application, and follow-up cultural procedures for the next few weeks after treatment.

Pesticides usually are applied with a pressure-tank sprayer, hose-end sprayer, drop spreader, or rotary spreader. For small lawns, when pests are not abundant, you might get by with an aerosol spray can.

Proper attire for applying pesticides includes a long-sleeve shirt, long pants, sneakers or work boots, and gloves.

PESTICIDE SAFETY Pesticide application is pretty straightforward, but there are risks to you and the environment. First and foremost, read the pesticide label. It will tell you what precautions to take, how to mix the product, which pests it will control, when to time the applications, and how to dispose of any leftovers.

In general, you should wear rubber boots (with no leather parts), unlined nitrile gloves (available at most garden centers, sometimes sold as "pesticide gloves"), long pants, and a long-sleeve shirt. While mixing pesticides, wear safety glasses or goggles and a rubber apron to guard against splashing. Rubber aprons are available through mail-order catalogs, farm-supply centers, and at some larger garden centers. After an application, fill the washing machine with hot water and launder the work clothes separately—never add them to the family laundry. After washing, let the washer run through its complete cycle again without any clothes.

PRESSURE-TANK SPRAYERS These sprayers are both flexible and relatively safe to use. Fill the tank with water and the prescribed amount of pesticide, screw on the lid tightly, and pump the plunger to build up pressure. You then hold the spray trigger with your dominant hand and pick up the spray tank with the other. The unit allows you to travel through the yard with ease, applying a small amount of pesticide exactly where it is needed; the pattern of delivery is relatively small, which increases accuracy.

HOSE-END SPRAYERS These units use the water pressure in a garden hose to disperse the contents of a spray bottle attached to the end of the hose. Place the recommended

PRESSURE-TANK SPRAYER

amounts of pesticide and water in the spray bottle, attach the sprayer to the hose, and turn on the water. The pesticide is diluted with water in the process.

A disadvantage of this system is that you may find it awkward to reach back to pull on the hose while trying to direct the spray. Because the spray pattern is quite large— 6 ft. to 8 ft. across—it tends to be wider than necessary and difficult to aim with accuracy. Finally, a drop in household water pressure can permit a backflow of pesticide into the home's water supply, potentially causing contamination.

SPREADERS AND SPRAY CANS You can use lawn spreaders to apply pesticides, particularly a granular product intended for subsurface problems such grubs or summer patch. Small and narrow areas, such as along driveways and sidewalks, are best treated with a drop spreader, while larger spaces can be covered more easily with a rotary model.

TURF TIP

Keep Pesticides in the Dark
Some pesticide formulations are altered by light so that they lose their power against pests. Store pesticides in a cool, dark place for longer shelf life.

Lawns That Bite Back

Breeders have been successful at developing perennial ryegrass and tall fescue with high levels of an endophyte, a naturally occurring insect pathogen that resists certain pests. These grasses are generally available at full-service garden centers.

Some pesticides are packaged in spray cans, and if you just have a few weeds or bugs, they work fine. You don't have to mix chemicals or deal with leftovers, which saves you time, but the tradeoff is that you'll pay considerably more per unit of active ingredient.

WHY PESTICIDES FAIL Despite our best efforts, bugs, weeds, and diseases are not always controlled with a pesticide application. Here are a few of the reasons for pesticide failure:

- **Microbial degradation.** Tiny soil-inhabiting microbes may feed on an insecticide, reducing the amount available to kill the target pest.

- **Volatilization.** A pesticide may evaporate from the grass or soil surface, reducing its effectiveness. Evaporation can also increase your exposure to volatile chemicals. You should avoid applying pesticides on a hot day, which increases the risk of getting a rash, dermatitis, or even internal poisoning.

- **Application errors.** The most common mistakes are caused by problems with the

equipment—clogged nozzles, gaps in coverage, and inadequate mixing of the pesticide with water in the spray tank. See the sidebar "Test Your Equipment" below.

- **Selecting the wrong pesticide.** There is no single cure-all pesticide. Check with your local cooperative extension office for the latest control recommendations on specific lawn and landscape pests.

- **Improper timing.** Each pest has a "stage of vulnerability" when it is most susceptible to a pesticide application, while other stages may make the pest virtually impossible to control. Learn what you can about the life cycle of pests that have become a perennial problem in your yard.

- **Inadequate irrigation.** This is a common problem when trying to control white grubs. Liquid formulations often dry on leaf blades without reaching the pests in the soil; the active ingredient in both liquid and granular formulations tends to be tied up by thatch before the ingredient can move down into the insect's feeding zone. Address this problem by selecting granular formulations for soil insects, watering the lawn before treatment, and making sure the product is watered-in after treatment. Consider core aeration to help chemicals penetrate the soil.

- **Using the wrong rate or formulation.** Be sure to follow the directions on the label thoroughly. Pay particular attention to the application rate for the target pest.

- **High water pH.** Did you know the quality of your water may cause pesticides to fail? Read product labels to check for a recom-

TEST YOUR EQUIPMENT

MAKE SURE SPRAYERS AND SPREADERS are up to snuff by performing simple calibration procedures on them before each application. Fill the sprayer tank with water, and spray a dry sidewalk on a warm day. Observe the spray pattern as it dries. It should be uniform; if not, clean out the nozzle or replace it.

Spreaders can malfunction in the same way. Test your spreader by applying fertilizer over the top of a tarp. If you see globs of product or scantily covered areas, adjust the spreader; if the problem persists, repair or replace the spreader.

mended pH range. An insecticide that performs well for several days at a pH of 5.5 may be effective for only several hours in alkaline water, and many parts of the country have water ranging up to a pH of 9.0 or 10.0. A simple water test will diagnose this problem. Contact your county or state health department for instructions on water testing. To offset alkalinity, you can mix in an acidic product sold for that purpose at garden centers.

Is It a Disease?

If you've looked high and low and can't find any insects to speak of, then disease may be the culprit. Diseases generally are much harder to identify because the causal organism isn't visible. In most cases, you would need a microscope to see the responsible fungus, bacterium, or virus. Bugs may be small, but at least you can see most of them.

Most lawn diseases make themselves known by their effects: as circular or irregular patches of browning grass, or as a generalized thinning and browning in various parts of the lawn.

It's important to consider a multitude of factors when controlling lawn diseases. The classic approach is to envision a triangle—with the host (in this case, the specific grass species and cultivar), the environment, and the pathogen itself as the three points. If any of these factors are not in place, then the disease won't be a problem. Yet, many diseases prevail because each of the points are in place.

Let's look at each of them. First, the environment. If your lawn is infected with pow-dery mildew, it's likely that it's not getting enough sunlight and air circulation. Your neighbor, on the other hand, may have good sunlight and air movement. So despite the fungus spores nearby, your neighbor doesn't see the disease.

Chapter 7 explains that there are hundreds of cultivars for each grass species. Some of them offer genetic resistance to diseases. If you're having trouble with a certain pathogen, one of the options for control is to simply change cultivars or species.

Is It a Weed?

You may be one of those homeowners who can live with a few weeds. But you should know that weeds are more than just a visual nuisance—they compete with lawn grasses for water, nutrients, space, and light. Even if you have elected to grow a low-maintenance lawn, you should spend some effort on weed control. These rugged plants have a way of taking over, so that you may end up mowing more weeds than grass.

A weedy lawn may also be a clue that your soil isn't up to snuff. Some weeds are opportunistic—they flourish on soils that won't support a lawn. Prostrate knotweed is a classic example because it tolerates compacted soils well. Take a close look at the hell strip between your sidewalk and the street—or the area between the hashmarks on a football field—and chances are you'll see many knotweed plants.

Lawns that are thin for various other reasons—leaf spot (melting out), greenbugs, shade—likely also have weeds. A thin lawn simply has many more openings for weeds

---

TURF TIP

Is it Another Problem ?

If none of the above bugs or diseases looks like the culprit, then consider the broad category of "other" problems. Areas with parallel stripes, large blotches of dead grass, stunted or wilted grass, or dead-looking grass are all likely caused by nonliving factors.

TURF TIP

Weeds Like a Crew-Cut Lawn

Mowing your lawn at a lower-than-recommended height can lead to a shallow root system and reduced leaf surface. Without a dense grass canopy, the lawn won't be as effective in shading out weeds.

to invade than a thick one. This is one of the disadvantages of a low-maintenance lawn: Weeds are a natural consequence of spending less time and less effort on a lawn.

Just about any plant can be thought of as a weed if it's not wanted in a certain location. In fact, Kentucky bluegrass ranks as a weed in a tall-fescue lawn because it has a different color, texture, and growth habit. The sight of few isolated interlopers doesn't have to be a call to action, just as a couple of fingerprints on a wall doesn't necessarily mean it's time to get out the paint and roller.

There are three basic methods of weed control: mechanical, cultural, and chemical. You'll want to use each at some point to have a good-looking lawn.

WEED HOE

Mechanical control

Removing weeds by hand is the simplest and most direct way to control them. You see a weed and you pull it—pretty straightforward. This works especially well for a small lawn or if you have children who need household chores. I remember many hot summer days pulling dandelions from the yard to earn a quarter from my dad. Unless you're paying your children a big fee, mechanical control is inexpensive and involves no chemicals.

A back-saving variation on pulling is to use a weed hoe. Its V-shaped head slices the weed in two. The disadvantage of either pulling or using a hoe is that the root may not be killed, allowing the weed to grow right back.

Cultural control

A thick, healthy lawn *naturally* discourages weeds from invading or germinating. Follow the sound, commonsense cultural practices outlined in chapters 1 through 5, and you'll set the stage for a dense, nearly weed-free yard. Proper mowing, aeration, wise cultivar selection, good drainage, fertilization, efficient irrigation—all of these strategies work together to help grass compete with weeds. Omit one or a couple and the lawn could suffer.

Chemical control

Due to advances in modern chemistry, there are many products on the market that can be used to kill or prevent weeds. If used responsibly, they can help you maintain a quality lawn. These controls fall into two basic categories: pre-emergence and post-emergence. There are some "organic" options for control of weeds. The most effective one is the pre-emergence herbicide, corn gluten meal. This does a reasonable (60 percent to 70 percent) job of preventing crabgrass, foxtail, and certain broadleaf weeds as well. Unfortunately, most organic weed-control products fall far short of customer expectations. Hand pulling and mechanical means, such as using a dandelion digger, remain good options for controlling weeds. As mentioned previously, when using any pesticide, be sure to read and follow explicitly all directions on the label.

PRE-EMERGENCE HERBICIDES These are preventive products, applied to the lawn before the weed shows up. Then, as the weed germinates, it absorbs the herbicide and dies before emerging aboveground. Use these herbicides primarily to control annual grasses, such as foxtail and crabgrass, and also annual broadleafs such as purslane and spurge. For maximum effectiveness, pre-emergence products need to be applied when soil temperatures are at least 50°F. In lawns with a history of heavy weed pressure, a second application in midsummer is recommended. After the product is on the lawn, help it to enter the soil by watering it in.

WHAT YOU'LL NEED
Applying Chemicals
✓ Protective clothing, including long sleeves, long pants, rubber boots, eyewear, and rubber gloves
✓ Pressure-tank or hose-end sprayer
✓ Appropriate herbicide or pesticide
✓ Dishwashing soap, if called for on the product label

Beware of Lawn Mushrooms

Mushrooms are related to the organisms that cause common lawn diseases. Some are quite attractive, but all should be avoided.

You may be thinking to yourself, "Wait a minute, I've hunted and eaten morel mushrooms before, and I'm still breathing." This may be true, but mushrooms found in a lawn are rarely the edible kinds, and they could well be highly poisonous. Don't eat them, and don't let your children so much as touch them. It's just not worth the risk.

Mushrooms commonly appear on a lawn a few days after a summer rainstorm. Fortunately, they are not harmful to the grass, other than providing a bit of a nuisance when mowing. There is no chemical application that will effectively control mushrooms, so just kick them over or practice your golf swing on them.

POSTEMERGENCE HERBICIDES These products are sprayed on the weed's leaves. Both broadleaf and grassy species can be targeted. To achieve maximum control and to minimize damage to the lawn, avoid mowing for a couple of days *before* application. This allows the weed time to produce enough leaf surface to absorb the herbicide fully. Then, don't mow for a couple of days *after* treatment to ensure that the herbicide has adequate time to penetrate the weed.

If the lawn is under stress from drought, heat, or insect pests, water it and delay herbicide treatment until the grass—and the weeds—have a chance to recover. When weeds are stressed, they are less able to absorb an herbicide. After the application, however, delay watering for a day or so to avoid washing the herbicide off the leaf surface of the weeds.

TURF TIP
What Weeds Say about Your Soil
Certain weeds are opportunistic—they flourish on soils that won't support a lawn. If you've got a lot of weeds, it may be a sign that your soil isn't up to snuff. Do some tests to find out.

SURFACE-FEEDING INSECTS

INVADER	DESCRIPTION	SYMPTOMS
Armyworms, cutworms, and fiery skippers	The larvae of these species eat the stems and leaves of grass plants.	The lawn appears dead in patches, but the problem is serious only if the pests are found in large numbers.
Billbugs	Newly hatched billbugs feed from within grass stems, hollowing them out and leaving a fine sawdust-like excrement.	The telltale sign of a billbug infestation is that stems easily break away from the roots when tugged. As the larvae mature, they begin feeding on roots as well, causing the lawn to appear drought stressed.
Chinch bugs	Mainly a pest of sorghum and other field crops, chinch bugs occasionally cause significant injury to lawns. They do damage both by extracting plant juices and by injecting a toxic saliva that disrupts the movement of water and nutrients within the grass plant.	The lawn develops a patchy area that yellows over time, then turns brown and dries out.
Clover mites, banks grass mites, and spider mites	Mites crawl around on grass blades, insert a mouthpart, and suck out plant juices.	Affected lawns show a general yellowing.
Greenbugs	Greenbugs, also known generally as aphids, feed by sucking plant juices, injecting toxic saliva in the process.	The damage often appears as an orange-colored circle of dying grass plants. A closer look may reveal that the insects are causing grass blades to curl around themselves as a means of protection from the sun and wind.
Leafhoppers	Walk out on the lawn in the evening and you're likely to see a few leafhoppers flying around.	Leafhoppers withdraw plant juices from grass blades but not in quantities sufficient to cause much trouble.

IDENTIFICATION	SOLUTION	
Some of the caterpillars are striped, some spotted; they often feed at night.	The best defense against these worms is a thick, healthy lawn that can outgrow the injury. In many yards, birds provide sufficient natural control by eating pests.	
Use the detergent test, and count the number of billbugs you find. It doesn't take too many to cause injury—only one or two per square foot can make trouble.	Chemical control is not recommended because the bugs feed inside the plant and are protected from spray applications. Instead, reseed with endophyte-enhanced grass cultivars (see the Turf Tip on p. 86) to replace the injured plants. Mark next year's calendar with a note to target the adults with a foliar treatment during the susceptible period, usually in midspring.	
To look for chinch bugs, remove both ends of a coffee can and push it a couple of inches into the affected lawn. Fill the can with water. If chinch bugs are present, they will float to the surface in a minute or two. (You may also notice them if you use the test with lemon-scented dishwashing detergent, described previously.)	Control these pests by reducing thatch and by overseeding with grass cultivars containing high endophyte levels (see the Turf Tip on p. 86). Consider applying a foliar insecticide for large numbers of chinch bugs (on the order of 20 to 30 per square foot).	
Mites are tiny, eight-legged critters (they're not true insects but close enough).	These mites only occasionally cause enough damage to warrant an insecticide or miticide application. The injury can be reduced by watering the lawn—to both disrupt their feeding and reduce moisture stress on the grass plants.	
You may need a hand lens to identify these insects. They are tiny and, being green, tend to blend in with the infested plant.	Follow good cultural practices and consider applying a foliar insecticide if damage spreads beyond a small patch.	
These bugs are wedge shaped, holding their wings in a pup-tent arrangement when at rest on a grass blade.	Leafhoppers may cause temporary injury, but if the lawn is healthy, it is usually able to outgrow the damage.	

UNDERGROUND-FEEDING INSECTS

INVADER	DESCRIPTION	SYMPTOMS
Sod webworms	If you see medium-size buff-colored moths flying around the lawn at dusk, then you may have webworms. The moths, with ½-in. wingspans, are the adults of larvae that burrow through the thatch at night to eat grass leaves and stems.	The first signs of webworms are small, ragged brown spots. Looking closer, you'll see a grazed or scalped appearance on the blades. If feeding continues, the patches merge to create areas of blighted lawn.
Earthworms	Although they do not feed on plant roots, earthworms can significantly disrupt the surface of a lawn.	In the process of moving through the ground, earthworms push soil and fecal material aboveground, where it hardens in bumpy globs. Eventually, the lawn may become so uneven that it is difficult to mow or to walk on barefoot.
Mole crickets	In the South, mole crickets can cause serious injury to bermudagrass, centipedegrass, and St. Augustinegrass lawns.	Crickets feed on grass roots and tunnel through the soil, causing adjacent roots to dry out and die. The dead grass pulls up quite easily, revealing the tunnels.
White grubs	In most parts of the country, white grubs are the number-one lawn pest.	The pests feed voraciously on turf roots, causing entire sections of the lawn to die. Grubs are the larvae of various beetles— Japanese beetles, black turfgrass aetenius, northern and southern masked chafers, and may (or june) beetles. Check for patches of dead-looking grass. This condition is often confused with drought stress. It also may be that you have *both* problems at the same time.

IDENTIFICATION	SOLUTION	
The lemon-scented detergent routine should help bring out the worms if present. They are gray to tan in color, with rows of black spots.	Healthy lawns usually are able to resist injury from sod webworms. However, if many of them are feeding on your lawn, consider applying a foliar insecticide. Mow the grass and remove the clippings before treatment for best results. Apply in the evening when the larvae are active, then water the area to help the insecticide penetrate through the thatch.	
Worms come up out of the soil after heavy rains. They are best identified by the material they leave on the surface.	To reduce the unevenness of the lawn, you can set a power rake on the high side and run it over the small mounds. See chapter 5 for more information on how to use a power rake. Although you can also smooth the surface by rolling the lawn when the soil is moist, that procedure tends to compact the soil. My personal suggestion is that you live with the worms. They are wonderfully beneficial organisms that naturally aerate and fertilize your lawn.	
These are relatively large critters, 1½ in. to 2 in. long. They look similar to common crickets, except that their head and front legs are a bit larger.	The most common control is to use a bait form of insecticide at the first sign of injury. Baits typically are pellets of an attractive material (often apple pumice or fruit extracts) impregnated with an insecticide; look for ones that are specially formulated for mole crickets. Repeated applications may be necessary to keep them at bay. Apply the bait at night for best results.	
Cut into the sod and peel it back to reveal the presence of the grubs. If they have been actively devouring the roots, the sod should roll up as easily as a piece of carpet.	A count of at least 5 to 10 grubs per square yard means you should consider an insecticide treatment. Because grubs tend to revisit in following years, it's best to mark your calendar for another application next year as a preventive measure.	

CIRCULAR AND IRREGULAR-PATCH DISEASES

DISEASE		DESCRIPTION
Brown patch		Circular patches of dead grass, from 6 in. to a few feet across.
Fairy ring		This disease produces large patches of affected grass, usually in rings measuring several feet in diameter.
Pythium blight		Pythium is most common on perennial ryegrass plants in lawns with a mix of grasses. It can be a problem when grass blades are continually wet and the soil has poor drainage.
Snow molds		This disease comes in two colors. Pink snow mold occurs in winter during prolonged cool, wet weather, especially where there has been cold drizzle, fog, and heavy wet snow. Gray snow mold is favored by extended periods of snow cover and aggravated when the lawn is compacted by walking or sledding.
Summer patch and necrotic ring spot		These closely related diseases cause exactly the same pattern of damage in the lawn and control is roughly the same, so we'll consider them together (even though a plant pathologist might scowl at us).
Take-all patch		Common in the Pacific Northwest, take-all patch looks similar to other patch diseases in that the roots are killed.

SYMPTOMS	SOLUTION
Brown patch produces roughly circular patches, somewhat similar to summer patch and necrotic ring spot but slightly larger in size. Upon close inspection, you'll notice that the leaves are blighted—speckled with blotches of off-color or bleached-out areas. In contrast, the roots and crowns are affected in summer patch and necrotic ring spot. Brown patch is favored by hot, humid nights when air circulation is poor. If you've had a few nights like that in a row, expect to see signs of the disease.	You can help prevent the disease by switching to a slow-release nitrogen fertilizer in early summer; this won't stimulate the soft, lush grass growth that is susceptible to infection. It also helps if you reduce thatch and follow other sound cultural practices discussed in chapters 4 and 5. In lawns with a history of brown patch, consider a foliar fungicide treatment at the first sign of symptoms. In most cases, only one or two applications are necessary, particularly if the weather turns cool and dry.
The rings are actually double, with an inner ring of dead grasses and an outer ring of particularly dark green grasses, which, oddly, may be growing faster than the healthy lawn around them. Mushrooms are often found growing in the dying rings.	Lawns with heavy thatch are more prone to fairy ring, as are those with buried pieces of decaying construction lumber or tree roots. The fungus grows on these materials, and you can help check the disease by heavily aerating or dethatching. To make the rings less noticeable, lightly fertilize the affected area so that it will turn a darker green. Most folks simply choose to live with fairy ring, as it's largely a cosmetic problem.
Look for patches of grass in which many individual blades turn brown and collapse. They often have a slimy or oily feel to them, and a fishy odor may be noticeable in the early morning. As with brown patch, the damage is heightened by warm nights, high humidity, and poor air circulation.	No single control measure is effective. It may help to increase air circulation by thinning or removing landscape plantings; to switch to low-release nitrogen fertilizers, in moderate amounts; to avoid walking on wet turf, especially at night; and to improve soil drainage by aerating the lawn.
Pink snow mold appears as roughly circular, rusty brown patches of various sizes. The grass blades can take on a salmon pink appearance when wet. Gray snow mold causes patches of grayish tan grass about a foot across, particularly where snow has been piled near driveways and parking lots.	Reduce snow-mold injury by waiting until the lawn is entering dormancy before putting on a winterizer application of fertilizer. This is the last application of the season, to be made after the lawn has stopped growing for the year. Consider installing snow fencing to divert drifting snow away from the lawn. If snow molds have been a problem for several years, you might apply a fungicide in late fall as a preventive measure.
Infected lawns appear pockmarked, with roughly circular areas of brown grass; often there is a tuft of healthy grass growing in the middle of the dead area. With heavy infestations, the areas merge to give the lawn a spotty brown appearance.	Remove thatch when it becomes excessive and overseed with disease-resistant grass cultivars. Although the fungus begins infecting the roots and crowns in cool weather, symptoms become visible, in the heat of summer; once the plants begin to die, there's not much you can do except rake out and reseed affected areas in the early fall. Consider taking preventive steps the following season, well before you'd see the symptoms.
You may notice a pockmarked appearance in the lawn. Check for depressed or sunken, roughly circular patches of blighted grass with a reddish bronze color. Cool, wet conditions in spring and fall favor the fungus's development.	Some relief can be had by maintaining a proper soil pH, below 6.5. The pH can be lowered if necessary with a balanced fertilizer program that includes sulfur or ammonium sulfate.

(continued on p. 96)

CIRCULAR AND IRREGULAR-PATCH DISEASES [CONTINUED]

DISEASE	DESCRIPTION
Dollar spot	Favored by warm days and cool nights, this disease is an easy one to identify on the lawn.
Leaf spot	This disease is apt to get a foothold in cool, moist weather.
Powdery mildew	The lawn takes on a dusty appearance that's hard to overlook.
Rust	The damage done by rust outbreaks varies widely from year to year; at its worst, the disease can leave a lawn severely thinned.
Slime molds	Suspect this one if your lawn takes on a dark gray cast.
Stripe smut	No, this disease is not something seen on XXX-rated pay-per-view television but a serious disease of lawns. The name refers to the lines of black fungus spores that appear on grass blades.

SYMPTOMS	SOLUTION
Dollar spot produces leaf lesions that appear as if someone had dropped a small amount of bleach on the grass blade. In the lawn, symptoms occur in a circular area about 3 in. across. From a distance, these spots can give the lawn an overall tan or rusty color.	Dollar spot is common on under-fertilized lawns, so a light application of slow-release fertilizer usually improves the appearance. Other sound, commonsense lawn practices are helpful as well.
Check for dark purplish brown spots on grass blades. As the disease progresses, the crowns and roots also deteriorate, preventing the normal flow of water and nutrients. From a distance, lawns infected with the disease take on a yellowed, beat-up appearance, with half or more of the leaves shriveled up in a way that could be described as "melting out."	Most newer grass cultivars have some level of genetic resistance; you can use them to prevent further infections. It also helps to water only in the morning hours, reduce thatch, and apply only slow-release nitrogen fertilizer. If your lawn has had heavy infections, consider applying fungicide before trouble recurs as a preventive measure.
Affected leaves turn yellow or brown in color as the disease progresses. Then, as the plants die, the lawn becomes thin.	Powdery mildew is encouraged by insufficient sunlight and little air circulation. You can remedy both conditions by pruning or removing shrubs and trees, and then reseed damaged areas. Another alternative is to switch to a fescue, St. Augustine, or centipedegrass. Or, if the lawn doesn't receive at least 3 hr. or 4 hr. of sun, just forget about grass altogether and plant a shade-loving ground cover instead. Consider preventive fungicide treatments for persistent problems.
If a stroll across the lawn turns your white sneakers a rusty shade of brown, orange, or red, then suspect this disease. A close look will reveal pustules with a finely granular or dusty substance on the grass blades and stems.	Rust usually occurs when warm days and cool nights cause a heavy dew on the lawn. Prevent problems by maintaining the lawn's vigor and by mowing regularly. Early-morning watering also helps to keep the plants moist without extending the effects of the dew. For affected lawns in a highly visible area, you might choose to spray with a fungicide.
A close inspection reveals a substance resembling fireplace ash on grass blades. Slime molds are spread by wind, watering, mowing, and recreational activities, but they sometimes appear in the lawn for no obvious reason.	Slime molds aren't particularly damaging to lawns, so no control measures are recommended. If they are cosmetically offensive, simply sweep them away with a broom or hose them down with a few sharp blasts of water to dislodge the dusty spores.
When many blades become affected, the lawn takes on a yellowed, stunted appearance in a generalized area, often in 6-in. to 12-in. spots. Cool weather favors the development of stripe smut.	Commonsense lawn care does little to discourage stripe smut. Rake the area thoroughly and reseed with improved cultivars. If the smut reinfects your lawn, apply a systemic fungicide for control. These products move through the conductive vessels of the plant, much like prescription medicines do in our bodies. Systemics can be hard to find in the garden center, so you may need to hire a lawn-care service for this application.

OTHER MALADIES

PROBLEM		DESCRIPTION
Chemical or fertilizer misapplication		Lawn chemicals can leave their mark if applied too heavily.
Compaction injury		Heavy foot or vehicular traffic can compress the soil, making it difficult for roots to grow.
Dog-spot injury		Not all lawn chemicals come from a sprayer or hopper.
Iron deficiency		The lawn's color can signal an imbalance of a key nutrient.
Mower-blade injury		You might think that a mower can do only good things for a lawn, but if the blade is dull, it tends to batter the little plants.
Roadside-salt injury		In spring, this problem may be evident along areas where salt has been used to melt ice and snow over the winter.

SYMPTOMS	SOLUTION
If your lawn shows a large geometric pattern—such as stripes, a wedge, or a circle—it may mean that too much or too little fertilizer or herbicide was applied. Most commonly, it's not the active ingredient but the carrier of the product that is responsible.	In serious cases, if the grass doesn't grow back, you may have to remove the affected soil to a depth of 6 in. to 8 in. and replace it. Otherwise, the lawn simply can be left alone to recover for a few months before reseeding.
Lawns may look as though diseased or insect infested, with a thin, stunted appearance. Grass often disappears altogether. The trouble comes about because compaction restricts the roots' ability to reach into the soil.	If the condition is serious, you may have to extensively aerate or till the affected soil, the seed a new lawn or re-establish the existing lawn. You can add organic matter to help prevent future injury, but restricting lawn traffic is the best remedy.
If the lawn is dotted with tufts of dark green grass in an otherwise normal-looking background, then chances are that Rover or Fluffy can take the credit. Urine and waste solids cause the turf to grow vigorously for a few days, then die from excess salts.	Not much can be done to alleviate this injury. You can try flushing the affected areas with large volumes of water, as well as lightly fertilizing to mask the symptoms. You may wish to install a fence to exclude neighborhood dogs. If *your* dog is the guilty party, check with your veterinarian; it is possible to add a supplement to the pet's diet, which will make its waste less harmful to the lawn.
Large areas of yellow turf may mean a lack of iron, particularly if a close inspection doesn't reveal the presence of stripe smut or other disease problems. The plants will become matted and difficult to mow in severe cases.	High-pH soils can make iron less available to plants, so test your soil as described in chapter 2. The soil test report should provide recommendations for improving the soil's fertility.
The lawn takes on a ragged appearance and becomes more vulnerable to foliar disease organisms.	Sharpen the blade monthly, ideally, or at least once per mowing season.
Affected areas look brown and stunted, while grass nearby appears unaffected.	Aerate the damaged areas and then flush them with frequent watering to leach out the salt. Prevent problems in the future by avoiding rock salt (sodium chloride). Instead, use calcium chloride salt in combination with sand to improve traction.

WEEDS

TYPE OF WEED		DESCRIPTION
Annual bluegrass		This bluegrass sounds like a desirable component of a seed mix, but it is classified as an annual grassy weed.
Black medic		Black medic, also known as yellow trefoil, is a warm-season annual broadleaf.
Blackseed plantain		The plantains are cool-season perennial broadleafs.
Buckhorn plantain		The plantains are cool-season perennial broadleafs.
Common chickweed		This winter annual broadleaf is indeed common and is favored by cool weather.
Crabgrass		Crabgrass is a well-known annual grassy weed. If left unchecked, it can become widespread in a lawn.
Dandelion		This cool-season perennial broadleaf is probably the best-known weed of all. It is harvested for spring greens, but do not pick the leaves from lawns that have been treated with chemicals.

IDENTIFICATION	SOLUTION
Annual bluegrass grows well in cool seasons and goes almost limp in the heat of summer. The lawn may take on a white cast from the seedheads if the plants are numerous.	You can prevent the recurrence of the weed by aerating soil that has become compacted. If you're able to identify the weed before the seedheads form, mow to prevent the plants from maturing. Problem areas can be spot-treated with Roundup and then reseeded.
Plants have small three-part rounded leaves and yellow flowers. This weed is difficult to tell apart from yellow woodsorrel (see p. 106).	Use broadleaf herbicides labeled for black medic.
The large round-to-oval leaves have prominent veins. Plants produce tall, thin seedheads.	Use postemergence herbicides labeled for plantain.
The medium-size oval-to-linear leaves are marked with prominent veins. The weed produces thin seedheads.	Use broadleaf herbicides labeled for plantain.
Note the medium green heart-shaped leaves and the tufted form. The flowers look like tiny white stars.	Use broadleaf herbicides labeled for common chickweed.
This weed is thick and has a coarse growth habit, taking on something of a crablike appearance. It germinates in late spring, when soil temperatures warm to at least 55°F. The weed succumbs to the first frost of the fall, as is typical of summer annuals.	Use pre-emergence herbicides for control.
The deeply notched leaves form a basal rosette, and large yellow flowers appear on stalks above the plant.	Use broadleaf herbicides labeled for dandelion.

(continued on p. 102)

WEEDS [CONTINUED]

TYPE OF WEED		DESCRIPTION
Field bindweed		This is a warm-season perennial broadleaf.
Foxtail		Foxtail is a familiar annual grassy weed that germinates in late spring.
Goosegrass		This annual grassy weed germinates in late spring.
Ground ivy		Ground ivy is a mat-forming cool-season perennial broadleaf.
Henbit		Henbit is a winter annual broadleaf.
Moss and algae		Mosses and algae are about as small and meek as an unwanted plant can get.
Mouse-eared chickweed		This chickweed species is a cool-season perennial broadleaf.

IDENTIFICATION	SOLUTION
Bindweed has medium-size, arrowhead-shaped leaves. It spreads aggressively through stolons.	Use broadleaf herbicides labeled for bindweed.
Look for the upright habit and the fuzzy seedheads that give the plant its name.	Use pre-emergence herbicides.
The plants have a flattened habit and silvery growth.	Use pre-emergence herbicides.
Look for rounded leaves and little lavender flowers. The plants spread by stolons.	In fall, use broadleaf herbicides labeled for ground ivy.
Identify this one by its rounded leaves, square stems, and pinkish purple flowers.	Use broadleaf herbicides labeled for henbit.
You're probably familiar with mosses—typically light green, low-growing plants that feel soft and velvety to the touch. Algae appears as a green to black, slimy layer over thin turf areas. Both are found most commonly on bare soils.	No chemical treatment is effective. You can experiment with raising or lowering soil pH to 6.5, but the best approach is to devote the area to something other than lawn.
The fuzzy, round-to-oval leaves give the weed its name. It occurs in patches in the lawn.	Use broadleaf herbicides labeled for mouse-eared chickweed.

(continued on p. 104)

WEEDS [CONTINUED]

TYPE OF WEED		DESCRIPTION
Nimblewill		Nimblewill is a warm-season perennial grassy weed.
Prostrate knotweed		Prostrate knotweed is a creeping cool-season annual broadleaf.
Purslane		Purslane is a warm-season annual broadleaf.
Quackgrass		Quackgrass is a perennial grassy weed.
Shepherds purse		This is a winter annual broadleaf.
Speedwell		Speedwell is a winter annual broadleaf.
Spurge		Spurge, or spotted spurge, is a warm-season annual broadleaf.

IDENTIFICATION	SOLUTION
This narrow-bladed grass is objectionable mostly in early spring and late fall in cool-season lawns.	There are no selective controls for the homeowner. Spot-treat with Roundup and reseed.
This weed germinates in early spring. The thin, wiry stems have small elliptical leaves. Prostrate knotweed grows well in compacted soils.	Use early-season applications of pre-emergence and postemergence herbicides labeled for knotweed. In many situations, complete renovation is necessary because this weed is so competitive. Treat it with Roundup, go over the area with a power rake, then reseed or resod.
Both stems and leaves are fleshy. The leaves are oval to rounded, green on top, and reddish brown underneath.	Use pre-emergence and postemergence herbicides labeled for purslane.
These coarse, wide-bladed plants spread through rhizomes.	There are no selective controls for the homeowner. Spot-treat with Roundup and reseed.
The leaves grow from a basal rosette, with a form something like that of a dandelion.	In fall, use broadleaf herbicides labeled for shepherd's purse.
Identify this one by its small, hairy, oval-to-rounded leaves and small blue-throated flowers.	Use pre-emergence and postemergence herbicides labeled for speedwell.
Spurge has small oval leaves, sometimes with a reddish spot in the center. You're apt to see this weed in hell strips, along driveways, and in other high-traffic, thin areas of the lawn.	Use pre-emergence herbicides or broadleaf herbicides labeled for spurge.

(continued on p. 106)

WEEDS [CONTINUED]

TYPE OF WEED		DESCRIPTION
Tall fescue		This fescue is classified as a perennial grassy weed, but it is a coarse and wide-blade species that is also grown as a lawn grass.
White clover		Despite the good luck associated with four-leaf clovers, the three-leaf variety of this cool-season perennial broadleaf can take over a lawn.
Wild violets		Violets are among the prettiest of plants to be classified as weeds. They are cool-season perennial broadleafs.
Yellow nutsedge		This nutsedge is an aggressive grassy perennial, especially if the area is often wet.
Yellow woodsorrel		This woodsorrel is a warm-season annual broadleaf.

IDENTIFICATION	SOLUTION
If fescue shows up in a bluegrass or bermudagrass lawn, it appears as a weed because of the difference in texture.	There are no selective controls for the homeowner. Spot-treat with Roundup and reseed.
The leaf shape is well known, as are the white or pinkish white flowers. Clover spreads through the lawn on stolons.	Use broadleaf herbicides labeled for white clover.
These violets have heart-shaped basal leaves and attractive white, blue, blue-and-white, or purple flowers. The plants don't take anything away from the appearance of the lawn if a few are scattered about.	If you have a large number of violets and can't enjoy them, use broadleaf herbicides labeled for the plant, making applications in the fall.
The grassy plants are light yellow to yellow green. They grow faster than most lawn grasses.	Although nutsedge is quite easy to pull, don't do it. Each stem is attached to an underground network of tubers, ready and waiting to grow when the weed is removed. Yank a nutsedge plant, and four or five will grow back in its place. Use broadleaf herbicides labeled for nutsedge.
Plants have small, pale green, heart-shaped leaves and yellow flowers.	Use broadleaf herbicides labeled for yellow woodsorrel.

THE GRASSES

UIZ YOUR NEIGHBORS ABOUT THE VARIETIES OF FLOWERS growing in their yard, and chances are they'll know. They may be able to tell you the tree species, as well. But ask about the varieties of lawn grass surrounding their home, and you're apt to get a puzzled stare. And yet the choice of grass cultivars is vital to having a great-looking lawn that isn't a weekend obsession.

A Quick Review

Start your decision-making process by thinking back to chapter 1, which encouraged you to determine just what your growing conditions are—sunny or shady, warm or cool, dry or damp, sandy or loamy, and so on. Then decide on the level of maintenance that you

(and your family) can live with. Together, these steps will suggest the grass or mixture of grasses that will suit you best.

Each grass variety has its own requirements, and the variety you pick has to be a good match with the lawn-care program you've chosen. A low-maintenance lawn may turn into something much more demanding

Choosing a grass species is a little like choosing a car. There are many choices, so you have to find the product that matches your needs.

if it is grown to a variety that needs more attention; by fertilizing and watering this variety sparingly, you're apt to invite drought stress and an invasion of weeds.

On the other hand, if you want the superb performance of a high-maintenance lawn but select a variety that likes a lean diet, the grass will grow excessively thick and lush, requiring frequent mowing. Overfeeding may also cause the lawn to become infected by any of several fungal diseases.

Selection factors

Grass, basically, is green. Beyond that, there are significant differences that you probably haven't taken the time to notice.

- **Color.** Yes, grass is green, but it comes in shades from light green to dark green, sometimes with a tinge of blue. Americans generally prefer deep green grasses, while Europeans prefer lighter lawns.

- **Leaf texture.** Coarse-textured grasses, such as St. Augustine, have wide leaf blades and a tough feel. Examples of thin, fine varieties are perennial ryegrass and fine fescue.

- **Density.** Density has to do with the number of grass plants per unit area. Grasses with high density ratings give the lawn a carpetlike appearance.

- **Growth habit.** Some cultivars are characteristically upright, while others are low growing and stay close to the soil surface. The more upright the growth, the more mowing you'll have to do. Some species such as tall fescue inherently have more

upright growth than low growers, such as Kentucky bluegrass, but plant breeders have developed dwarf tall fescue varieties.

- **Uniformity.** A grass that is uniform in color, texture, density, and growth habit will be pleasing to the eye and is preferred by most homeowners.

- **Disease and insect resistance.** Varieties are rated by their genetic ability to resist or overcome disease and insect attacks. Also, naturally occurring, pest-repelling fungi, called endophytes, live within certain tall fescue, fine fescue, and perennial ryegrass varieties. (See "Lawns That Bite Back" on p. 86.)

- **Drought resistance.** If you live in a dry area, investigate varieties that maintain their green color and good quality during prolonged drought.

- **Water-use efficiency.** Cultivars vary greatly in the amount of water they need to maintain an acceptable level of quality. Tall fescue is an example of a heavy drinker.

- **Heat and cold tolerance.** This considers a grass's ability to survive extreme winter and summer temperatures.

- **Rate of establishment.** Some grasses are quick to sprout and cover the ground, while others require patience. A fast grower will do a better job of resisting weed invasion, controlling erosion, and recovering from disease or insect damage.

- **Recuperative potential.** How fast will a grass grow back and return to health after

TURF TIP

Winter Overseeding

You can add perennial ryegrass to your lawn before warm-season grasses, such as bermudagrass and zoysiagrass, lose their green color in late fall. Especially in the South, this procedure keeps the lawn looking green though the cold months.

TURF TIP

Going Native

Most grass varieties grown on American lawns are from abroad, and they tend to need some coddling to do well in our various climates. Look into native grasses for alternatives that can do a better job of standing on their own, in terms of water needs, fertilizing, and mowing frequency.

Just as some ornamentals are shade adapted, certain turf species tolerate shade better than others.

COMMON MISTAKE

Miracle Grasses

Beware of ads claiming to offer a miracle grass that uses little or no water, never needs mowing, and withstands heavy use in a deeply shaded area. The perfect, universal cultivar has yet to be developed. For now, we have to do our best with grass blends that require us to spend discretionary time mowing and primping.

an injury? Some, such as Kentucky bluegrass and bermudagrass, have good recuperative potential. Tall fescue and perennial ryegrass are some that lack the ability to replace damaged stems, which means you'll have to reseed damaged areas.

- **Shade tolerance.** If you have trees of any size, you'll want to consider the light requirements of grass varieties.

- **Traffic and wear tolerance.** In heavily used lawns, a grass needs to be able to handle the compacting of the soil and to grow back over worn areas.

- **Thatch production.** Some grasses produce thatch faster than soil microorganisms can decompose it, meaning you'll need to periodically thin this layer. Diseases and insects tend to thrive in

thatch, and thatch also prevents water from reaching the roots. Heavy thatch producers include bermudagrass, St. Augustinegrass, Kentucky bluegrass, and zoysiagrass.

- **Nutrient-use efficiency.** Just as some people find they gain weight on a moderate diet, certain grasses use nutrients more efficiently than others.

Alternatives to Grasses

While true grasses are the most common lawn choices, certain low-growing broadleaf plants are also suitable. Although some folks label wild violets or white clover as weeds, an entire yard of them can be very attractive.

These broadleaves have several advantages. First, they require little maintenance. As you probably have observed, periods of neglect favor the clover and violets in your lawn; they grow quite nicely without lots of water or fertilizer. A second desirable feature is their slow growth rate—they rarely need mowing. Finally, they add color to a lawn when blooming. Waves of purple, blue, and white are refreshingly beautiful, particularly when set against a solid green background of shrubs.

If you live in southern California, consider dichondra. This plant produces rounded to heart-shaped leaves in a matlike appearance. It has fairly good shade tolerance but requires quite a bit of attention with fertilizer, water, and pest control to keep it looking healthy.

Coming Up with Your Own Blend

You don't have to go to the bother of mixing and matching your own grass formula because premixed, prepackaged products are available at any garden center. But if you take a particular interest in the plant varieties growing in your yard—flowers, shrubs, and trees—you might want to try customizing a blend of lawn grasses.

From a technical standpoint, a blend is a combination of several cultivars of the same species, while a mixture is a combination of cultivars of more than one species. Even though these terms may sound essentially the same, the distinction is important when selecting a lawn grass.

Several grasses are blended or mixed to gain the best qualities of each component. For example, if you're choosing varieties for a somewhat shady lawn with the relatively cool growing season of northern Pennsylvania, you might combine improved cultivars of Kentucky bluegrass and fine fescue. The bluegrass would thrive in the sun, and the fescue would take over in the shade. You also could come up with a blend—using several cultivars of tall fescue, for example—again building in adaptation to sun and shade.

Violets are sometimes regarded as an intrusive weed, even though they have attractive heart-shaped leaves and pretty blossoms. A patch of them can be treated as a welcome accent in the lawn.

Coastal and Mountain Grasses

If you live along a shoreline or up on a mountain, consider planting the lawn with a cool-season grass, with its preference for considerable rainfall and moderate temperatures.

There is one disadvantage to these alternatives—a low tolerance for traffic. Even the mildest-mannered kids or dogs may eventually trample them and spoil their appearance, so they are best used in areas with little traffic.

Which Grass Is Best?

In general terms, grasses are divided into warm- and cool-season varieties. The cool-season grasses are generally grown in areas where frosts and freezing temperatures are routine for a significant portion of the year, while warm-season grasses are favored in regions where mild to hot weather predominates. Buffalograss, zoysiagrass, and creeping bentgrass are exceptions in that they can be grown successfully in both cool and warm regions.

Cool-season grasses

To get the benefit of the strong points of two or more cultivars, you can use a mixture of seed. In general, only cool-season grasses are blended (see the next section), such as

A good ground cover can be just as effective as grass in providing contrast, void, and a neutral color.

RATING COOL-SEASON GRASSES

Grass Species	Shade Tolerance	Disease Resistance	Wear Tolerance	Nitrogen Requirement	Heat Tolerance	Drought Tolerance	Recovery Potential
Kentucky bluegrass	Fair	Variable	Good	Variable	Fair	Good	Excellent
Rough bluegrass	Good	Fair	Good	Low	Poor	Poor	Good
Tall fescue	Good	Good	Good	Low	Good	Excellent	Poor
Fine fescue	Good	Good	Fair	Low	Good	Good	Poor
Perennial ryegrass	Fair	Variable	Excellent	Medium	Good	Fair	Poor
Creeping bentgrass	Fair	Fair	Poor to fair	Medium	Fair to good	Fair	Good

RATING WARM-SEASON GRASSES

Grass Species	Shade Tolerance	Disease Resistance	Wear Tolerance	Nitrogen Requirement	Heat Tolerance	Drought Tolerance	Recovery Potential
Common bermudagrass	Fair	Fair	Good	Low	Fair	Excellent	Excellent
Improved bermudagrass	Fair	Variable	Excellent	Medium	Poor	Excellent	Excellent
Zoysiagrass	Good	Fair	Good	Low	Good	Excellent	Good
Centipedegrass	Fair to good	Fair to good	Fair	Low	Poor	Good	Poor
St. Augustinegrass	Good	Fair	Fair	Low	Poor	Good	Good
Buffalograss	Fair	Excellent	Fair	Very low	Good	Excellent	Fair

Kentucky bluegrass with perennial ryegrass or chewings fescue with hard fescue. These grasses are similar to each other and compatible in terms of leaf texture and growth habit (see "Coming Up with Your Own Blend" on p. 113).

Warm-season grasses

Unlike cultivars suited to cooler climates, warm-season grasses are seldom planted in mixtures because they lack compatibility and just don't look right when blended.

TURF TIP

Herbicides Can Hurt Grass, Too

Many broadleaf weed-control products contain 2,4-D, which can damage a zoysia lawn breaking dormancy in spring or a St. Augustine lawn at any time.

COOL-SEASON GRASSES

KENTUCKY BLUEGRASS

The most widely grown cool-season grass is the well-known Kentucky bluegrass.

- Medium-textured, green to dark green lawn of good density.
- Aggressive sod-forming habit attributable to its strong rhizome development.
- Ability to spread into thin areas makes it a good choice for reviving stressed lawns.
- Some cultivars are pest susceptible.
- Fair high-temperature tolerance and good to excellent cold-temperature tolerance.
- A related cultivar—rough bluegrass—tolerates wet and somewhat shady sites.

TALL FESCUE

The toughest cool-season grass species is turf-type tall fescue.

- The coarsest texture of any cool-season grass, as well as the lowest shoot density.
- It resists insect feeding and has an extensive root system that efficiently draws on soil moisture, making it a good candidate if pests and drought are problems in your area.
- Fair cold-temperature tolerance and good to excellent heat tolerance.
- The recuperative potential is quite low because it does not spread laterally.

FINE FESCUE

The group is made up of hard fescue, sheep fescue, creeping red fescue, and chewings fescue.

- Medium to dark green.
- Needle-fine texture.
- Except for creeping red fescue, these do not spread significantly.
- Exhibit good to excellent shade tolerance.
- Best use is in a mix with shade-tolerant cultivars of bluegrass, sown in areas that receive 3 hr. to 6 hr. of sun per day.

PERENNIAL RYEGRASS

Perennial ryegrass is commonly mixed with Kentucky bluegrass to improve wear tolerance, allow growing in shade, and speed up establishment.

- Shiny, medium to dark green, and fine to medium in texture.
- Does not spread laterally.
- Tolerant of both cold and warm temperatures.
- Germinates rapidly, making it useful if you need to get a lawn off to a fast start, as when the grass is injured a couple of weeks before you plan to throw a backyard party.

CREEPING BENTGRASS

Used primarily on putting greens but also could be considered if you want to put in a specialty lawn for boccie or croquet.

- Very low, very fine-textured grass.
- Spreads quite readily through rhizomes.
- Susceptible to a wide range of fungal diseases; along with a need for frequent mowing, it is considered a high-maintenance cultivar.
- Good cold-temperature tolerance and fair heat tolerance.
- Used primarily on putting greens but also could be considered if you want to put in a specialty lawn for boccie or croquet.

WARM-SEASON GRASSES

BERMUDAGRASS

Bermudagrass is one of the most widely used and rugged warm-season species.

- Common bermudagrass is a bit coarse, having medium texture, while hybrid bermuda is medium to fine.
- All bermudas are aggressive spreaders, so that they establish themselves quickly and will bounce back when damaged.
- Tolerates close mowing.
- Does well in a wide range of soil types.
- Cold-temperature tolerance is poor; heat tolerance is good.

ZOYSIAGRASS

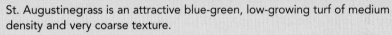

With its deep root system, zoysiagrass can avoid drought stress in many situations.

- Medium texture and medium green.
- Low growing and tolerates a low mowing height.
- Grows through rhizomes and stolons.
- Typically has better cold tolerance than bermudagrass, as well as excellent heat tolerance.
- Grows slowly and is quite stiff and tough.

CENTIPEDEGRASS

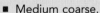
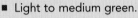

Centipedegrass is good, tough turf if you are after a low-maintenance lawn.

- Light to medium green.
- Medium coarse.
- Low maintenance.
- Spreads by short, leafy stolons to form a mat of low-growing stems and leaves.
- Poor cold-temperature hardiness but good heat tolerance.
- Poor recuperative potential, due to its slow growth rate and modest spreading ability.
- Average shade tolerance, better than that of bermudagrass.

ST. AUGUSTINEGRASS

St. Augustinegrass is an attractive blue-green, low-growing turf of medium density and very coarse texture.

- Spreads rapidly by stolons and has a medium-deep root system that allows for rapid establishment and good recuperative potential.
- Poor low-temperature tolerance limits usage where frost commonly occurs; heat tolerance is good.
- Handles shade better than any other warm-season variety.

BUFFALOGRASS

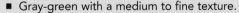

One of the few lawn grasses native to the United States is buffalograss, the quintessential low-maintenance, warm-season turf. (Even Kentucky bluegrass is an imported species.) It is adapted to the central United States—from Texas north to Minnesota, and Colorado east to Illinois.

- Gray-green with a medium to fine texture.
- Typically open density, although newer cultivars grow more thickly.
- Excellent pest resistance.
- Once established, buffalograss doesn't have to be watered unless you're going through a drought, and it has a very low fertility requirement.
- Good to excellent cold and heat tolerance.
- Because it is slow growing and slow to establish, it has a limited ability to recuperate from stress or injury.
- Best suited to low-maintenance lawns.

CHAPTER 8

LAWN CALENDARS

E VERY PART OF THIS GREAT LAND has its own challenges and special nuances for growing grass. And within each region, there are many pockets of uncharacteristic localized conditions. For example, Texas residents know that Dallas is different from El Paso in terms of rainfall, sunlight, temperature, and humidity. Elevation differences strongly influence how Colorado homeowners tend their lawns in Yuma compared to those in Estes Park. States with coasts on the ocean or the Great Lakes also may see big differences.

This chapter gives generalized lawn calendars for each region. I suggest you find the one for your area, photocopy it as a handy reference, and nail it to the wall of the garage or storage shed where you keep lawn equipment.

These calendars are general in nature and will have to be adapted for your local conditions. In other words, they're a good place to start. A range of a few weeks may be provided to allow for variations in the zones. Along the northern edge of each zone, the latter part of the time period indicated will be more appropriate, while residents

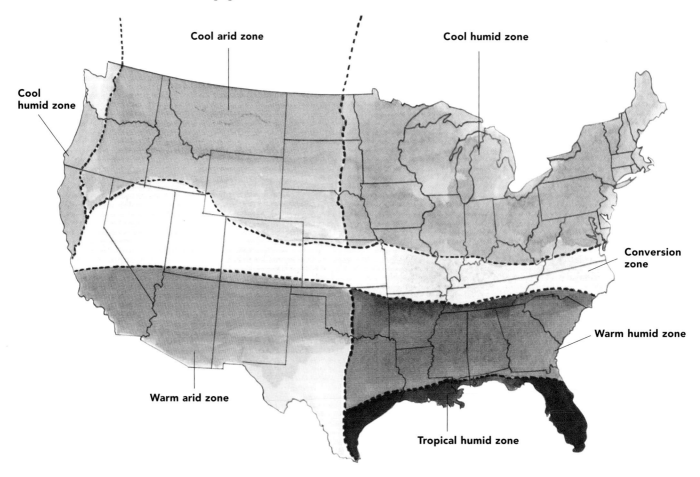

along the southern edge should focus on the earlier part of the range. Additionally, in order to show all the possible times for each activity, they are set up for a medium- to high-maintenance regime. Refer to earlier chapters for suggestions on caring for your lawn with minimal input.

Note that all the figures on nitrogen fertilizers are for actual nitrogen to be used per 1,000 sq. ft. and that slow-release nitrogen fertilizers are preferred.

Cool Humid and Cool Arid Zones

The cool humid zone is characterized by cool to cold winters and mild to hot summers. Actually, there are two zones: the Pacific Coast area west of the Cascade Mountains from southern British Columbia to northern California; and the northeast to north central region of the United States, along with the adjacent provinces of Manitoba, Ontario, Quebec, and New Brunswick. These areas typically receive 25 in. to 45 in. of rainfall a year.

Cool-season grasses predominate in this region, including Kentucky bluegrass, perennial ryegrass, fine fescue, tall fescue, and rough bluegrass (see the chart on pp. 124–125). Tall fescue is favored toward the southern edge of the region because its lack of winter hardiness limits its survival to the north. Other cool-season grasses that are appropriate include smooth brome, timothy,

orchardgrass, and redtop. And don't rule out warm-season turfgrasses such as zoysiagrass, commonly found toward the southern edge, and buffalograss, used for low-maintenance lawns especially in the north central region (see the chart on pp. 126–127).

The cool arid zone is made up of the Rocky Mountains and the Great Plains, with large differences between the two in elevation. The climate is normally continental, with hot summers and cool to cold winters. Annual rainfall varies from 10 in. to 25 in. and is heaviest in spring and summer.

Kentucky bluegrass is the predominant species; fine fescue is used in the drier areas with supplemental irrigation. Buffalograss, native to this area, is grown commonly as a low-maintenance grass. Other natives that are occasionally used include blue gramagrass, sideoats gramagrass, and crested wheatgrass. Bermudagrass and zoysiagrass find use along the southern edge of this zone, particularly in Kansas (see the charts on pp. 124–127).

Warm Arid Zone

This climatic zone comprises a wide belt from southern California to west Texas. Rainfall ranges from less than 5 in. to 20 in., with low humidity and lots of sunshine. Most grasses require supplemental irrigation to survive.

Not many turfgrasses are well adapted to this zone, with St. Augustinegrass, bermuda-

TURF TIP

Going Native

If you want to reduce maintenance, take a cue from nature and install plants that perform well on their own in nature preserves and parks.

grass, and zoysiagrass seen in most lawns (see the chart on pp. 128–129). Alternatives include bahiagrass and kikuyugrass, and there is increased interest in buffalograss, particularly in Arizona and southern California.

Warm Humid Zone

Mild winters and hot, hot summers typify the warm humid zone. High humidity and rainfall are the norm; annual amounts range from 30 in. in northeast Texas to 45 in. along the Atlantic seaboard to 70 in. along the eastern Gulf Coast.

Bermudagrass is the turf of choice for most Southerners in the warm humid zone, while zoysiagrass is commonly grown in the northern part of the region (see the chart on pp. 130–131). Kentucky bluegrass and tall fescue are also grown along the northern edge, although they struggle in hot summers. Other warm-season species grown in the zone include St. Augustinegrass, bahiagrass, and carpetgrass, primarily in the southern one-third of the zone.

Tropical Humid Zone

This is the warmest region, extending from the southeast coast of Texas and the southern edges of Louisiana, Mississippi, and Alabama to most of Florida. This zone is noted for heavy rainfall and hot, humid summers. Centipedegrass, St. Augustinegrass, and carpetgrass are the primary species selected for low- or medium-maintenance lawns, while hybrid bermudagrass is favored for high-maintenance yards (see the chart on pp. 132–133).

Conversion Zone

This is no-man's-land, where temperatures and humidity converge to form a transitional zone between the major areas of grass adaptation. In this area, there are no hard-and-fast rules. The best choices are species that grow well in the northern edges of the warm humid and the warm arid zones and the species that are suited for the southern parts of the cool arid and cool humid zones. Tall fescue and zoysiagrass are the most commonly grown grasses in the conversion zone.

If you live in a transition zone, find the zone closest to you and proceed from there. You may have to use some information from the zone charts to the north and the south of you.

Grass doesn't belong in every part of the landscape, so consider the benefits of shade-adapted perennials and ground covers.

COOL HUMID AND COOL ARID ZONES

	April	May	June	July
FERTILIZING	Apply ½ lb. nitrogen.		Apply ½ lb. to ¾ lb. nitrogen.	Avoid fertilization.
WATERING	Apply supplemental water in absence of rain, for total of 1 in. per week.		Apply supplemental water in absence of rain, for total of 1¼ in. per week.	Apply supplemental water in absence of rain, for total of 1½ in. per week.
WEED CONTROL	When soil temperatures reach 55°F, apply pre-emergence herbicide for crabgrass, goosegrass, and foxtail.	Control broadleaf weeds such as dandelions. Make second pre-emergence application, particularly if weed pressure is great.		
INSECT CONTROL		Apply foliar insecticide for control of adult billbugs if a problem in the past.	Scout lawn for sod webworms, and control if necessary. Apply preventive insecticide for white grubs if a problem in the past.	
DISEASE CONTROL	Scout lawn for leaf spot, and control if necessary. When soil temperatures reach 62°F to 65°F, apply systemic fungicide to parts of lawn with history of necrotic ring spot and summer patch.			
THATCH REMOVAL	Check thickness of thatch. If more than ⅝ in., dethatch. Consider application of leaf-spot fungicide after thatch removal.			
AERATION	Aerate compacted lawns.			
OVERSEEDING	Overseed thin lawns with improved cultivars.			

COOL-SEASON GRASSES

	August	September	October	November	
Fertilizing	Avoid fertilization.	Apply 1 lb. nitrogen.	Apply 1¼ lb. to 1¾ lb. nitrogen. Apply a winterizer formulation.		
Watering	Apply supplemental water in absence of rain, for total of 1½ in. per week.	Apply supplemental water in absence of rain, for total of 1 in. per week.	Apply supplemental water in absence of rain, for total of 1 in. per week.		
Weed Control		Control broadleaf weeds.			
Insect Control	Scout lawn for white grubs, and control if necessary.				
Disease Control		Scout lawn for leaf spot, and control if necessary.			
Thatch Removal		Check thickness of thatch. If more than ⅝ in., dethatch. Consider application of leaf-spot fungicide after thatch removal.			
Aeration		Aerate compacted lawns.			
Overseeding		Overseed thin lawns with improved cultivars.			

COOL HUMID AND COOL ARID ZONES

	April	May	June	July
Fertilizing		Apply ½ lb. nitrogen after spring green-up.	Apply ½ lb. nitrogen.	
Watering		Apply supplemental water in absence of rain, for total of 1½ in. per week.		Apply supplemental water in absence of rain, for total of 1½ in. per week.
Weed Control	When soil temperatures reach 55°F, apply pre-emergence herbicide for crabgrass, goosegrass, and foxtail.	Control broadleaf weeds such as dandelions. Make second pre-emergence application, particularly if weed pressure is great.		
Insect Control			Scout zoysia lawns for chinch bugs, and control if necessary. Scout buffalograss lawns for mealybugs, and control if necessary.	
Disease Control	Scout zoysia and buffalograss lawns for leaf spot. If symptoms are widespread and in early stages of development, consider a fungicide application.			Scout zoysia lawns for brown patch, and control if necessary. Scout zoysia and buffalograss lawns for summer patch. Consider treatment in early summer the following season.
Thatch Removal			Check thickness of thatch. If more than ⅜ in., dethatch.	
Aeration			Aerate compacted lawns.	
Overseeding			Plant plugs to thicken weak lawns.	

WARM-SEASON GRASSES

August	September	October	November	
				FERTILIZING
Apply supplemental water in absence of rain, for total of 1½ in. per week.				WATERING
	Control broadleaf weeds.			WEED CONTROL
Scout warm-season lawns for white grubs, and control if necessary.				INSECT CONTROL
Scout zoysia and buffalograss lawns for summer patch. Consider treatment in early summer the following season.				DISEASE CONTROL
				THATCH REMOVAL
				AERATION
				OVERSEEDING

WARM ARID ZONE

	Feb./March	April	May	June
FERTILIZING	Apply 1 lb. nitrogen.		Apply 1 lb. nitrogen.	
WATERING	Apply supplemental water in absence of rain, for total of 1 in. per week.			Apply supplemental water in absence of rain, for total of 1¼ in. per week.
WEED CONTROL	When soil temperatures reach 55°F, apply pre-emergence herbicide for crabgrass, goosegrass, and foxtail.		Spot-spray with broadleaf herbicide to control perennial weeds as needed.	
INSECT CONTROL	Inspect lawn for armyworm and mite injury, and treat as necessary.			
DISEASE CONTROL	Scout bermudagrass, bahia, and St. Augustine lawns for symptoms of spring dead spot. Replant as necessary.	Scout St. Augustine lawns for symptoms of take-all root rot disease. Consider renovation or a change in fertilizer source if called for.		Scout zoysia lawns for symptoms of brown-patch disease, and control if necessary.
THATCH REMOVAL			Check thickness of thatch. If more than ⅝ in., dethatch.	
AERATION			Aerate compacted lawns.	
REGRASSING				Plant plugs to thicken weak lawns.

	July/August	September	October	November	
Fertilizing	Apply 1 lb. nitrogen.				
Watering	Apply supplemental water in absence of rain, for total of 1¼ in. per week.	Apply supplemental water in absence of rain, for total of 1 in. per week.		Periodic watering may be required, especially in winters that are warmer than normal.	
Weed Control	Spot-spray with broadleaf herbicide to control perennial weeds as needed.		Routinely inspect lawn for newly sprouted weeds and spot-spray as needed (through January).		
Insect Control	Scout for white grubs, especially where previous injury has occurred, and treat as necessary.				
Disease Control					
Thatch Removal					
Aeration	Aerate compacted lawns.				
Overseeding					

WARM HUMID ZONE

	Feb./March	April	May	June/July
FERTILIZING	Apply 1 lb. nitrogen after spring green-up.		Apply 1 lb. nitrogen.	Apply 1 lb. nitrogen.
WATERING	Apply supplemental water in absence of rain, for total of 1 in. per week.			Apply supplemental water in absence of rain, for total of 1¼ in. per week.
WEED CONTROL	When soil temperatures reach 55°F, apply pre-emergence herbicide for crabgrass, goosegrass, and foxtail.		Spot-spray with broadleaf herbicide to control perennial weeds as needed.	
INSECT CONTROL	Inspect lawn for mole-cricket damage, and apply bait insecticide for control.		Apply foliar insecticide for control of adult billbugs if a problem in the past. Scout lawn for chinch bugs, and sod-webworm and armyworm injury, and control if necessary.	Apply preventive insecticide for white grubs if a problem in the past.
DISEASE CONTROL	Scout lawn for cottony blight, leaf spot, and dollar spot, and control if necessary.			Inspect lawn for brown patch and gray leaf spot, and control if necessary.
THATCH REMOVAL			Check thickness of thatch. If more than ⅝ in., dethatch.	
AERATION			Aerate compacted lawns.	
REGRASSING				Plant plugs to thicken weak lawns.

	August	September	October	November	
Fertilizing		Apply 1 lb. nitrogen			
Watering	Apply supplemental water in absence of rain, for total of 1¼ in. per week.	Apply supplemental water in absence of rain, for total of 1 in. per week.		Periodic watering may be required, especially in winters that are warmer than normal.	
Weed Control	Spot-spray with broadleaf herbicide to control perennial weeds as needed.		Routinely inspect lawn for newly sprouted weeds, and spot-spray as needed.		
Insect Control	Inspect lawn for mole-cricket damage, and apply bait insecticide in early evening for control. Scout lawn for chinch bugs, and control if necessary. Scout lawn for sod-webworm and armyworm injury, and control if necessary. Inspect lawn white-grub injury, and control if necessary.				
Disease Control	Inspect lawn for brown patch and gray leaf spot, and control if necessary.				
Thatch Removal					
Aeration	Aerate compacted lawns.				
Overseeding					

131

TROPICAL HUMID ZONE

	Feb./March	April	May	June/July
FERTILIZING	Apply 1 lb. nitrogen after spring green-up.		Scout lawn for iron deficiency, and apply ferrous sulfate if soil tests indicate a need. Apply 1 lb. nitrogen.	Apply 1 lb. nitrogen.
WATERING	Apply ¾ in. water in absence of natural rainfall, then wait for lawn to show signs of wilting before next watering.			Frequent, intense rainfall normally occurs during this period, so irrigate only as needed to prevent drought.
WEED CONTROL	When soil temperatures reach 55°F, apply pre-emergence herbicide for lespedeza, spurge, crabgrass, goosegrass, and foxtail.		Use caution when applying broadleaf herbicides, especially during drought stress. Hand pulling is preferable.	
INSECT CONTROL		Inspect lawn for mole-cricket damage, and apply bait insecticide in early evening for control. Scout lawn for chinch bugs, and control if necessary. Apply foliar insecticide for control of adult billbugs if a problem in the past. Scout lawn for sod-webworm and armyworm injury, and control if necessary. Apply preventive insecticide for white grubs if a past problem.		
DISEASE CONTROL	Scout lawn for cottony blight, leaf spot, and dollar spot, and control if necessary.			Scout lawn for pythium blight, and control if necessary. Inspect lawn for brown patch and gray leaf spot, and control if necessary.
THATCH REMOVAL		Check thickness of thatch. If more than ⅜ in., dethatch.		
AERATION			Aerate compacted lawns.	
REGRASSING			Plant plugs to thicken weak lawns.	

	August	September	October	November	
FERTILIZING		Apply 1 lb. nitrogen.			
WATERING	Frequent, intense rainfall normally occurs during this period, so irrigate only as needed to prevent drought.	Apply ¾ in. water in absence of natural rainfall, then wait for lawn to show signs of wilting before next watering.			
WEED CONTROL	Use caution when applying broadleaf herbicides, especially during drought stress. Hand pulling is preferable.		Inspect lawn for newly sprouted broadleaf weeds, and spot-spray as needed (through February).		
INSECT CONTROL	Inspect lawn for mole-cricket damage, and apply bait insecticide in early evening for control. Scout lawn for chinch bugs, and control if necessary. Scout lawn for sod-webworm and armyworm injury, and control if necessary. Inspect lawn for white-grub injury, and control if necessary.		Continue to inspect for white grubs, armyworms, and mole crickets, and control if necessary.		
DISEASE CONTROL	Scout lawn for pythium blight, and control if necessary. Inspect lawn for brown patch and gray leaf spot, and control if necessary.				
THATCH REMOVAL					
AERATION	Aerate compacted lawns.				
OVERSEEDING					

Appendix: Lawn-Care Companies

IT MAY BE DIFFICULT for you to find the time for lawn care, even though you enjoy being outside doing something with immediate, visible results. Or perhaps you're just less than thrilled with the prospect of carrying out all of the tasks necessary to having an attractive lawn.

If so, give some thought to turning all or part of the job over to a lawn-care company. In addition to the convenience, homeowners may find that their yards look better than ever. Lawn-care personnel tend to keep up with current developments in grass cultivars, fertilizers, and disease and pest control.

What to expect

Firms may offer a complete maintenance program, sometimes called "gardener service," for which they visit every week. Others only stop by a few times a year to apply fertilizer and control pests, leaving you to do the mowing, aeration, power-raking, and maintenance of the irrigation system. This minimal level may mean that occasionally you'll be faced with insect and disease problems.

No lawn-care company can promise a perfect lawn, especially when temperature, precipitation, and humidity fall out of the optimal range for the grass being grown. But then you won't be out that much money.

Annual charges range from $200 to $350, depending on the level of service provided and the part of the country you live in. To put these figures in perspective, the average do-it-yourself homeowner spends $70 to $100 per year on lawn-care products—seed, fertilizer, and pest control—not including the cost of a lawn mower, fertilizer spreader, or watering equipment.

Services

Just what can you expect the lawn-care service to do? Fertilizing is a basic part of any program. Most companies will also offer pre-emergence control (for crabgrass) and post-emergence control (for broadleaf weeds) as part of their standard package, although these may be extra-cost options. Many programs include control of surface-feeding insects (chinch bug, billbug, sod webworm) as well, while offering grub control at an additional cost. And some companies offer no insect control at all. Disease control is generally an optional service.

Low-maintenance plans

Your ideal may not be a lush green lawn that you'd be proud to host a wedding reception on. It could be that as long as the yard looks respectable, you're satisfied. If that's the case, choose a company that will customize an inexpensive low-maintenance regimen. You might ask them to apply a third of the normal rate of fertilizer with each application, and explain to them that you'll tolerate some pest and disease damage before control measures are resorted to.

LEVELS OF LAWN-CARE SERVICE

Service Plan	Low Care	Medium Care	High Care
Fertilization	1–2 times/yr.	3–4 times/yr.	3–4 times/yr.
Weed control	Pre-emergence	Pre-emergence	Pre-emergence
Mowing	None	Weekly	As needed
Insect and disease control	None	Grub control	As needed
Thatch removal	None	None	As needed
Aeration	None	Yearly	Twice a year

Resources

Books

Baxendale, Fred and Roch Gaussoin, editors. *Integrated Turfgrass Management for the Northern Great Plains.* Lincoln, Neb.: UNL Cooperative Extension, 1997.

Buchanan, Rita. *Taylor's Master Guide to Landscaping.* Boston: Houghton Mifflin, 2000.

Editors, *Better Homes and Gardens. Step-By-Step Landscaping.* Des Moines: Meredith, 1994.

Editors, *Fine Gardening. Garden Tools and Equipment.* Newtown, Conn.: The Taunton Press, 1990.

Editors, *Fine Gardening. Healthy Soil.* Newtown, Conn.: The Taunton Press, 1990.

Hendrix, Howard. *Reliable Rain.* Newtown, Conn.: The Taunton Press, 1990.

Giroux, Philip, editor. *Landscaping for Dummies.* New York: Hungry Minds, 1999.

Olkowski, Helga. *The Gardener's Guide to Common Sense Pest Control.* Newtown, Conn.: The Taunton Press, 1996.

Von Trapp, Sarah Jane. *The Landscape Makeover Book.* Newtown, Conn.: The Taunton Press, 2000.

Magazines

BACKYARD FARMER
byf.unl.edu

FINE GARDENING ®
www.taunton.com

HORTICULTURE®
www.hortmag.com

Sprinklers

HUNTER® INDUSTRIES
1940 Diamond St.
San Marcos, CA 92069
(760) 471-9626
www.hunterindustries.com
RAIN BIRD® CORP.

145 North Grand Ave.
Glendora, CA 91741
(626) 963-9311
www.rainbird.com

THE TORO® CO.
DIY Irrigation
8111 Lyndale Ave. South
Bloomington, MN 55420
(800) 367-8676
www.toro.com

Power mowers, trimmers, and edgers

ARIENS® CO.
655 West Ryan St.
PO Box 157
Brillion, WI 54110
(920) 756-2141
www.ariens.com

DEERE® & CO.
One John Deere Pl.
Moline, IL 61265
(309) 765-8000
www.deere.com

EXMARK® MFG. CO.
Industrial Park N.W.
Box 808
Beatrice, NE 68310-PO
(402) 223-6300
www.exmark.com

HONDA POWER EQUIPMENT® GROUP
4900 Marconi Dr.
Alpharetta, GA 30005
(800) 426-7701
www.hondapowerequipment.com

MTD®
Cleveland, OH 44136
(800) 269-6215
www.mtdproducts.com

SNAPPER®, INC.
Customer Relations
535 Macon St.
McDonough, GA 30253
(800) 935-2967
www.snapper.com

THE TORO CO.
Consumer Div.
8111 Lyndale Ave. South
Bloomington, MN 55420
(800) 348-2424
www.toro.com

CLEAN AIR GARDENING
5200 Martel Ave., #6Q
Dallas, TX 75206
(214) 370-0530
www.cleanairgardening.com

PROMOW®, INC.
8318 Clinton Park Dr.
Fort Wayne, IN 46825
(877) 477-6669
www.4apromow.com

SUNLAWN
326 Garfield St.
Fort Collins, CO 80524
(970) 493-5284
www.sunlawn.com

Fertilizers, pesticides, and seed

PRAIRIE FRONTIER
W281 S3606 Pheasant Run
Waukesha, WI 53189
(262) 544-6708
www.prairiefrontier.com

THE SCOTTS® CO.
Marysville, OH 43041
(800) 543-TURF
www.scotts.com

SEEDLAND®, INC.
9895 Adams Rd.
Wellborn, FL 32094
(386) 963-2080
www.seedland.com

Photo Credits

© Robert Black, University of Florida—pp. 44, 117 (from top: third photo)

© R. L. Brandenburg—p. 93 (from top: second, third photos)

© Robert C. Clark—p. 11

© John Fech—pp. 7, 16, 17, 18 (from top: second, third, fourth photos) 27, 28, 31, 33, 41, 48, 50, 61, 62, 66, 68, 72, 96 (from top: third photo), 98 (from top: first, third, fifth, sixth photos), 102 (from top: third photo), 104 (from top: first, fourth, sixth, seventh photos), 106 (from top: first, third, fourth photos), 113, 116 (from top: fifth photo), 117 (from top: first, second, fourth, fifth photos)

© V. A. Gibeault—p. 98 (from top: fourth photo)

© David Goldberg—p. 104 (from top: second photo)

© Saxon Holt—pp. 6, 38

Vincent Laurence, courtesy *Fine Gardening* magazine, © The Taunton Press, Inc.—p. 116 (from top: first through fourth photos)

© Douglas Linde—p. 98 (from top: second photo)

© Allan Mandell—p. 81

© J. Paul Moore—pp. ii, 12, 21, 23, 24, 100 (from top: third, sixth photos), 109, 112, 114, 119, 123

© Jerry Pavia Photography, Inc.—pp. 19, 65, 78

© Pam Peirce—pp. 100 (from top: first, fifth, seventh photos), 102 (from top: first, second, sixth, seventh photos), 104 (from top: third, fifth photos), 106 (from top: second, fifth photos)

© Susan A. Roth—pp. 5, 35, 53, 58, 71

© Steve Silk—pp. 1 (right), 15, 29, 39, 43, 45, 67, 110

© Lauren Springer—p. 18 (top and bottom photos)

Amy Rapaport, courtesy *Fine Gardening* magazine, © The Taunton Press, Inc.—pp. 1 (left), 54, 56, 63, 74, 75, 77, 84

© L. E. Trenholm, University of Florida—pp. 100 (from top: fourth photo), 102 (from top: fifth photo)

© University of Nebraska, Department of Entomology—pp. 82, 91, 93 (except second and third from top

© University of Nebraska, Department of Plant Pathology—pp. 94, 96 (except third from top)

© Tom Voigt, University of Illinois—pp. 102 (from top, fourth photo)

© Lee Anne White—pp. 13, 59

Rosalind Loeb Wanke, courtesy *Fine Gardening* magazine, © The Taunton Press, Inc.—p. 73